Thirty Days to MELODY

Ready-to-use Lessons and Reproducible Activities For the Music Classroom

By Betsy Henderson

Table of Contents

I0808909

ISBN 978-0-634-05421-1

HAL•LEONARD® CORPORATION
7777 W. BLUEMOUND RD. P.O. BOX 13819 MILWAUKEE, WI 53213

MOTIF • 1

INTRODUCTION

Name ______________________________

If you let a mel - o - dy in - vade your mind,
It may stay a long time, if it is the right kind.
Cir - cling 'round for ho - urs as you go a - bout the day,
but where it comes from, how it goes,
No one can say.

WHAT IS MELODY?

Melody is an organized sequence (order) of notes. You might be surprised to realize that you can recall hundred of melodies. The more often you hear a specific melody, the better your music memory will be. Even melodies without words are remembered. Recalling some random notes from the twelve available would be much more difficult than remembering your phone number, if not for an arrangement that catches your attention and interest.

1. Read the poem inside the box above as a group, using the rhythm notation and a steady beat to help you stay together.
2. Have one volunteer read the poem alone adding expression and emphasis on important words.
3. Have five confident volunteers add their own original melody, each singing one line of the poem at a time.

HISTORICAL PERSPECTIVE

Pictures and writings prove that music has existed for thousands of years. Much of the early music was created in chanting style, called **plainsong**, with little noticeable melody.

Because there was no system of notation established, music was not written down in the earliest form. Therefore songs were passed down from one generation to the next by simply singing and teaching songs to others. Therefore, music has always been an important part of social and family life in many countries.

ELEMENTS OF MELODY

As you know, a melody is a succession of musical sounds, or a specific order of notes. In this study, you will be working closely with the following important characteristics of a melody:

- Melodic pitches can move scale-wise (steps) or in larger leaps (skips).
- Melodic pitches can move upward (ascend), downward (descend) or remain the same.
- Melody has shape, form, rhythm and range.
- Melodies have beginnings, endings and direction.

MELODIC TYPES

Most music has melody, whether simple or complex. Described below are the three most common types of melodies:

1. A **motive** is the smallest melodic figure upon which a total composition is based. This important figure may occur in varied stages throughout the piece and is used as building material. (See **Bonus Question** below.)
2. The **tune** is a popular name for the melody that is easily remembered and sung. For example, a folksong, symphonic theme or popular songs on the radio all have tunes that are easily remembered.
3. A **theme** is a melody containing a main idea that is developed further in a composition, usually easily recognizable when it reappears and considered the subject of the composition.

BONUS QUESTIONS:

1. Do you recognize this familiar melodic motive? Can you name the famous classical composer who created it and the name of the piece?

____

____

____

2. Tell in your own words why you think a melody is called the soul of music?

____

____

____

MOTIF • 2

VOCABULARY

Name ____________________

MELODY VOCABULARY

The twenty words listed below will help make your study of melody more meaningful and productive. Follow these suggestions as you become familiar with these important terms.

1. Read through the following list of words, placing a check mark by the terms you can already define from any previous study based on music theory.
2. Look each word up in a dictionary for a more detailed and in-depth definition.
3. Highlight each of these vocabulary words as they appear in upcoming lessons.
4. Add five more words of your own to this list, as they are used in activities from the lessons.
5. Choose the ten most familiar words to you from the list and use each of them in written sentences.

MELODIC READINESS VOCABULARY

Accidental – chromatic sign which alters the pitch of a single tone within a measure (♯ - sharp, ♭ - flat, ♮ - natural).

Cadence – musical punctuation signaling the end of a musical phrase or section.

Chromatic – tones foreign to a given key or scale or all tones of a chromatic scale built entirely on half steps.

Conjunct – a melodic line that moves in a step-wise progression.

Contour – direction of a melody or series of pitches.

Disjunct – a melodic line that moves in larger leaps (skip-wise) from one to another.

Interval – pitch distance between two notes.

Major – "greater" with respect to the quality of an interval, scale, chord, key tonality or mode.

Minor – "lesser" with respect to the quality of an interval, scale, chord, key tonality or mode.

Modulation – change of key signature within a composition.

Motive – a short, distinctive melodic pattern.

Pentatonic – a major scale without the fourth and seventh tones, making it a five-tone scale.

Phrase – a small section of composition comprising a complete musical thought.

Pitch – highness or lowness of a tone determined by the frequency of vibrations.

Octave – an interval of two tones which spans eight scale degrees (C to C or F to F).

Ostinato – repeated melodic or rhythmic pattern.

Range – distance between the highest and lowest pitches in a melody.

Register – the relative lowness or highness of a whole melody.

Scale – graduated series of tones arranged in a specified order (CDEFGABC).

Tessitura – general average pitch level of a melody.

MATCHING TERMS

Put the letter of the word in the right column that best matches the numbered term in the left column:

_____1. interval	a. change keys
_____2. octave	b. repeated pattern
_____3. pentatonic	c. tone series
_____4. scale	d. shape
_____5. phrase	e. vibration
_____6. accidental	f. five-tone scale
_____7. contour	g. low C to high C
_____8. ostinato	h. distance
_____9. modulate	i. sharp
____10. pitch	j. section

SCRAMBLED TERMS

Using the vocabulary list, unscramble these terms:

1. V T N R I L A E = ___ ___ ___ ___ ___ ___ ___ ___
2. R N O U O C T = ___ ___ ___ ___ ___ ___ ___
3. H S E P R A = ___ ___ ___ ___ ___ ___
4. T E M V O I = ___ ___ ___ ___ ___ ___
5. A O T S O T I N = ___ ___ ___ ___ ___ ___ ___ ___

In these blanks, write the number of syllables in each word you unscrambled above:

a. __________ b. __________ c. __________ d. __________ e. __________

FILL IN THE BLANKS

1. A five-tone scale is called a ______________________________ scale.
2. An ______________________________is the pitch distance between two tones.
3. The highness or lowness of a tone is called its ______________________________.
4. ______________________________ is the distance between the highest and lowest pitches in a melody.
5. A sharp, flat or a natural are examples of ______________________________.

BONUS QUESTIONS

1. What is the difference between conjunct and disjunct melodies?

____

2. Which two numbered tones of the major scale are missing in a pentatonic scale?

____

METHODS • 3

COMPARABLES

Name ______________________________

COMPARE ONE WITH ANOTHER

The melody or tune of a musical composition can be recalled long after the song is heard or performed. As a melodic line moves along from any note, the next pitch will go higher (upward), lower (downward) or stay the same. In this lesson you will learn about the aspects of a melody that deal with **high/low**, **skips/steps** and **same/different**.

HIGH/LOW PITCHES

Pitch is determined by the number of vibrations per second that a sound produces. The faster the vibration, the higher the pitch. Pitch is measured by how many sound waves are produced in a second.

German scientist, Heinrich Hertz (1857-1894) is known for standardizing the measurement of sound vibrations. The 'A' above middle 'C' on a piano vibrates 440 times in a second as measured by Hertz, so 'A440' became the international pitch standard in 1939 from which all other pitches are determined. In contrast, the lower left key on a piano (A) moves at 27.5 vibrations per second while the note played at the right end of the keyboard (C) can move up to 4,000 vibrations per second. Middle C on the piano vibrates at 261.6 vibrations per second.

Try these High/Low exercises:

1. Open the lid of a grand piano (or the top of an upright piano) and observe the mechanism inside as the piano is played. Notice how thick the lower strings are, how thin the upper strings are and what happens when the strings are struck by the felt hammers.
2. Hidden from your view, your teacher or student volunteer will play various notes on the piano or barred instrument. Touch your head when you hear a high pitch, touch your toes when you hear a low pitch and touch your waist when you hear a pitch in mid-range.
3. As a class, make a list of sounds from everyday life that are high (whistles) and low (thunder).
4. Select five melody bells of different pitches and five students to represent these pitches. While one student plays the five pitches slowly in order from lowest to highest, the five students will arrange themselves from lowest (sitting on the floor) to highest (standing with arms raised). Try playing the bells in a mixed up order as the students rearrange to visually match the sounds.

STEPS/SKIPS

In the previous lesson you learned that melody lines that move primarily in a step-wise way are called **conjunct** melodies and are easily sung. In the example below, notice how the noteheads in the first two measures move in a step-wise manner:

Melodies that move in skips or leaps are called **disjunct** melodies, adding the difficulty of large intervals to perform. In this example, circle the noteheads in measures 2-3 and 6-7 as they move with more distance between them:

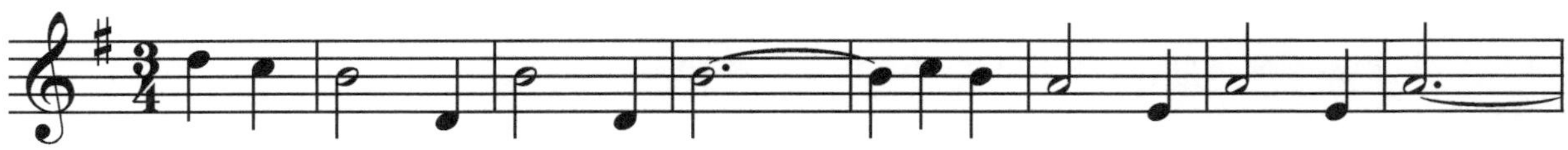

SAME/DIFFERENT

It is usually a simple process to recognize qualities of sameness within a melody or differences in a tune or rhythm. In the examples below, find which one shows repeated notes (same) ______, which one shows identical repeated phrases (same) ______ and which one shows nothing repeated (different) ______.

Ex.1

Ex. 2

Ex. 3

BONUS QUESTIONS

1. What is the function of an *oscilloscope* and how does it work?

____

____

2. What does the term *perfect pitch* mean and how is it demonstrated?

____

____

PHRASE / CONTOUR

Name ______________________________

PHRASING

A listener doesn't have to take in a whole melody at once, because melodies are divided into sections called **phrases**, which are complete musical thoughts. Think of phrases as musical sentences.

The word **cadence**, taken from a Latin word meaning to fall, is the term given to the resting place at the close of a phrase. Many compositions have four-measure phrases that are common, but not exclusive as segments. You will notice that short phrases can echo each other, repeat themselves or contrast each other.

1. In the example below, the curved lines above the staff show you where the phrases are set to give meaning to the text.

As you sing the song, move your right hand in the air from left to right to show the length of each phrase, making an arc or rainbow shape in the air.

2. In the next example, show where the phrases should be by drawing curved lines above the staff.

As you sing the song, move your right hand in the air from left to right making the phrase arcs with your hand. Check to see that your phrasing matches the flow of the text.

Find a familiar song with phrase markings from a music textbook and sing the song using the lines as clues for taking breaths.

CONTOUR

The upward and downward movement of the pitches used creates the **contour** or shape of a melody. The highest note of a melody is considered its **focal point**.

1. Using the example below, follow the noteheads (circles on the staff) to determine the contour of the melody. Do the lines move conjunctly or disjunctly?

Hush, Lit-tle Ba - by, don't say a word, Pa-pa's gon-na buy you a mock-ing bird,

2. Notice that the noteheads would look like this pattern if removed from the staff.

Hush, Lit-tle Ba - by, don't say a word, Pa-pa's gon-na buy you a mock - ing bird,

3. Draw the noteheads for this song on your own below, and then connect them, like a 'dot-to-dot' to show the contour of this melody.

Melodies tend to move toward an obvious highpoint, called the **climax** of a piece. A musical climax is achieved when a dramatic melody reaches a peak of interest, not always at the end of the composition.

BONUS QUESTIONS

1. Listen to or sing "The Star-Spangled Banner" to determine where the musical climax occurs. Write the lyrics of the phrase in which it occurs and circle the most important word.

____

____

____

2. Choose a song from your music textbook without phrase markings and decide how many phrases are needed to define the text.
3. Find a song in a hymn book and decide where phrase markings would be needed.

METHODS • 5

RHYTHM

Name ______________________________

BEAT/RHYTHM

Rhythm represents the heartbeat of a song and is a basic element of music along with melody. A melody would not be organized into clearly defined segments without the accompanying sense of rhythm. In fact, most melodies could not exist without an underlying structure of rhythm, which gives them their total character.

As the melody moves upward and downward, the rhythm catches our focus and gives life to the composition. So, after finding the steady beat (a pulse that is continuous), find the rhythm of the words (patterns of sounds that move evenly or unevenly).

1. Sing a familiar song, tapping the steady beat in your feet as you clap the rhythm of the words with your hands.
2. Face a partner having one person tap a steady beat with the right hand on their partner's left hand, while the other person taps the word rhythm with their right hand on the partner's left as you sing a familiar song.

RHYTHM SYLLABLES

A good place to begin reading rhythm notation is by using the rhythm syllables below that were created by Zoltan Kodály, a Hungarian composer/teacher (1882-1967). With a quarter note (ta) getting one beat, review these rhythm syllables:

= ta (1 sound per beat)	= ta-ah-ah (3 beats)
= ti ti (2 sounds per beat)	= tika tika (4 sounds per beat)
= rest (one beat of silence)	= tika ti (1 beat)
= ta-ah (2 beats)	= ti tika (1 beat)
= ta-ah-ah-ah (4 beats)	= syn-co-pa (2 beats)

NOTE VALUES

As you get more acquainted with printed music, you will discover that a note's duration is determined by how it appears on the staff. Notes have a circular part called a notehead (o •) that may be attached to a stem (|) and may have flags (♪) or connecting beams (⊓).

Ex.

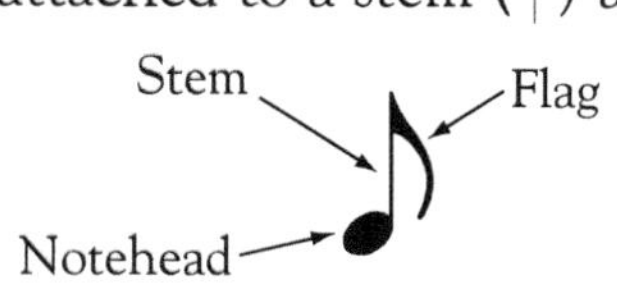

Ex.

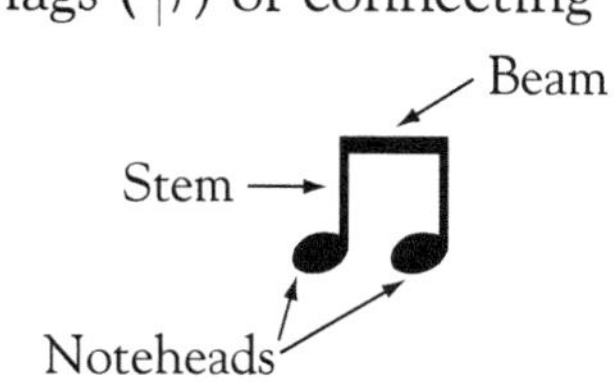

This chart will help you learn about the most commonly used notes, corresponding rests and how many beats duration they receive in $\frac{4}{4}$ meter.

> A whole note (𝅝) or whole rest (𝄻) lasts for four beats.
>
> A half note (𝅗𝅥) or half rest (𝄼)lasts for two beats.
>
> A quarter note (♩) or quarter rest (𝄽) lasts for one beat.
>
> An eighth note (♪) or eighth rest (𝄾) lasts for one-half of a beat.
>
> A sixteenth note (𝅘𝅥𝅯) or sixteenth rest (𝄿) lasts for one-fourth of a beat.

DOTTED NOTES

If a note or rest has a dot after it, that note/rest is made longer by half the value of the note/rest itself. For example, a dotted half note (𝅗𝅥.) gets three beats in $\frac{4}{4}$ meter because the half note is worth two beats plus an additional beat for the dot.

Circle the dotted notes below and tell the number of beats given each one:

TIED NOTES

Using a curved line called a **tie**, notes of the same pitch can be joined. The first note is sounded and then held for the duration of both notes, without the second note being sounded again.

Tell how many beats these tied notes get in $\frac{4}{4}$ meter above.

BONUS QUESTIONS

1. Say aloud what kind of note each one is in this example, then put the note value under each note in $\frac{4}{4}$ meter:

2. Circle the dotted note and the tied notes.

TIME SIGNATURES

Name ______________________________

WHAT IS A TIME SIGNATURE?

A **time signature** is found at the beginning of the first line of music, following the clef sign and key signature (sharps or flats). Used as a symbol to tell how many beats will be found in every measure, the time signature has certain patterns of beats that are stressed or unstressed. To find the time signature of a piece, look in the designated place for two numbers, one on top of the other.

The top number tells us how many beats are contained in each measure and the bottom number tells what kind of note gets one beat.

3 Number of beats per measure
4 Quarter note (♩)gets one beat

If a 2 is the bottom number, a half note (𝅗𝅥) will get one beat or if an 8 is on the bottom, an eighth note (♪) gets one beat.

Beats are grouped by measures that are divided appropriately by vertical bar lines

PRACTICE MAKES PERFECT

Fill in these answers for what the top and bottom numbers tell about the music in each instance.

Ex. **3** = ______________________________
2 = ______________________________

Ex. **3** = ______________________________
4 = ______________________________

Ex. **6** = ______________________________
8 = ______________________________

WHAT, NO NUMBERS?

If instead of two numbers, a capital C in place of the time signature is a shortened way of showing a 4/4 time signature or **common time**. Because so much music, especially popular Western music, is written in 4/4 meter, the C is used as a quicker way to signal this time signature. If the C has a vertical line through it, (₵), this is the symbol for **cut time** or 2/2 time, meaning that each note gets half its original value.

 (Common)

 (Cut)

The term **meter** also refers to time signatures and to the way beats are grouped. The three types of meter are:

duple – two beats per measure in a strong – weak pattern

triple – three beats per measure in a strong – weak – weak pattern

quadruple – four beats per measure in a STRONG – weak – strong – weak pattern

MATCH THEM UP

Draw a line from the time signature on the left to the correct example on the right.

2/4 (Duple) 

3/2 (Triple) 

4/4 (Quadruple) 

FILL IN THE TIME

In the following musical examples, look at the number of beats and notes in each measure and write the correct time signature at the beginning of each staff following the clef-sign and key signature.

METHODS • 7

SCALES

Name ______________________________

If you learn to play an instrument, you will become very familiar with musical scales as you work toward nimble fingers and quick thinking. **Scales** are arrangements of pitches in stair step order from lowest to highest or from highest to lowest. In our Western culture, the two most common scales are called **major** and **minor**.

MAJOR SCALES

Major scales are comprised of eight sequential notes, beginning and ending on the same letter, since only seven letters are available for use in music:

A B C D E F G

(then start over again!)

A **major** scale has half steps between the 3rd and 4th notes and between the 7th and 8th notes. This applies to any major scale in any key. Look at the diagram below to see where the half steps are. All other intervals in a major scale are whole steps.

H = Half step – the smallest interval. On the piano, half steps are between two keys that are next to each other. (Ex. B to C or D to D#)

W = Whole step – two half steps. On the piano, whole steps are between two keys with a key in between. (Ex. C to D or G to A)

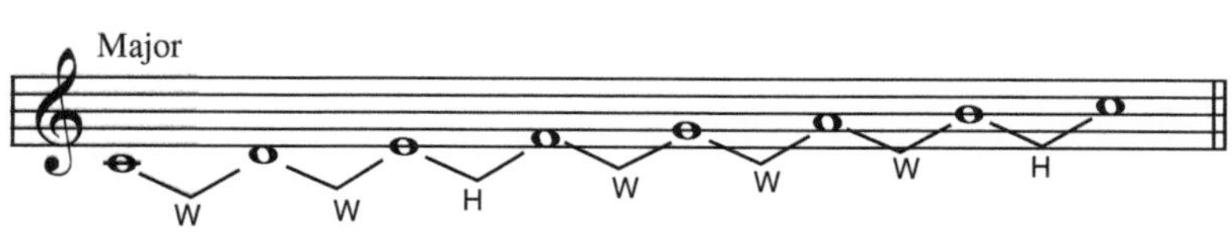

In the C Major scale, starting on the note C, only white keys on the piano are used. Look to see where the half steps are on the keyboard

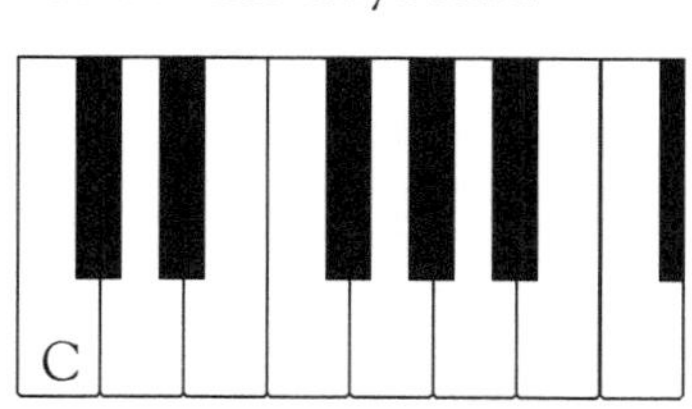

Number the pitches from one to eight and put in the absolute letter names from low C to high C.

MINOR SCALES

In arranging major scales, we start on the **tonic**, which in the first note of the scale or the keynote. For example, a B Major scale starts on the note B (the tonic). Minor scales also center on their tonic, but their half steps occur in different places. There are three kinds of minor scales: **natural**, **harmonic** and **melodic**.

1. **Natural Minor** – the half steps occur between the 2nd and 3rd notes and the 5th and 6th notes and uses the same notes going upward and downward.

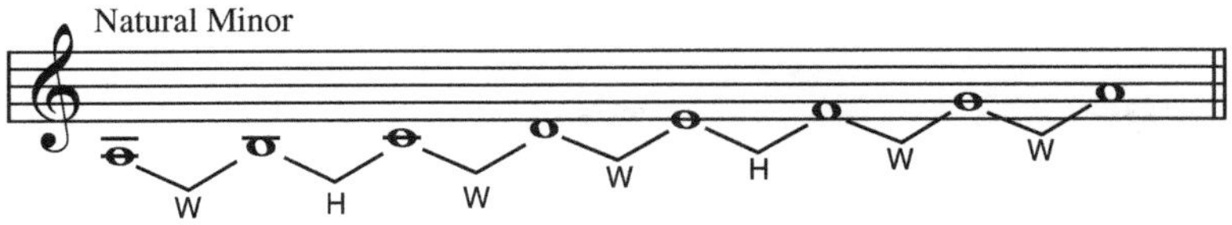

2. **Harmonic Minor** – the same notes as a natural minor scale, except the 7th note is raised a half step on the way up and on the way down.

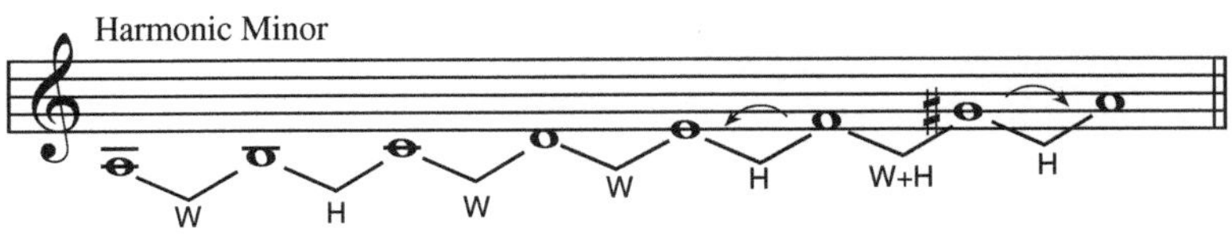

3. **Melodic Minor** – the same notes as a natural minor, except the 6th and 7th notes are raised a half step on the way up the scale and are lowered to their original pitches on the way down the scale.

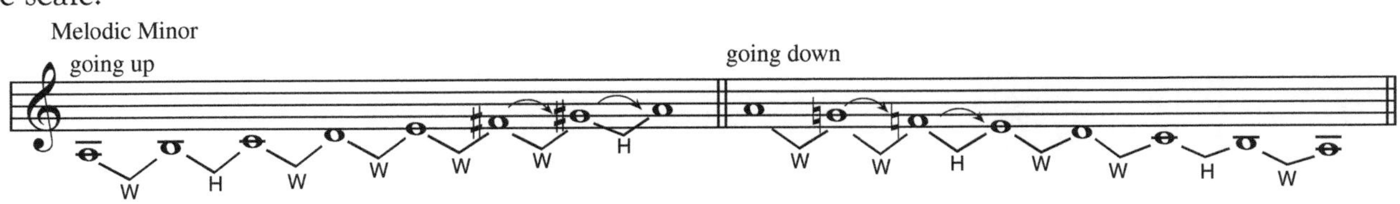

PENTATONIC SCALE

A **pentatonic scale** is a scale of only five notes, taking the major or minor scale and omitting the 4th and the 7th notes of the scale.

Label these pentatonic scales with the letter names of each note.

C Pentatonic

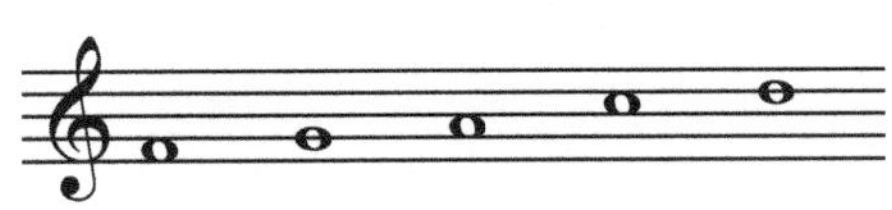

F Pentatonic

G Pentatonic

Next, draw and label the missing 4th and 7th notes in each key above.

Now, play a pentatonic scale, using only black keys on the piano, starting on G flat.

CHROMATIC SCALE

A **Chromatic Scale** uses all twelve consecutive half steps in an octave, starting on any note, then moving in an upward or downward direction.

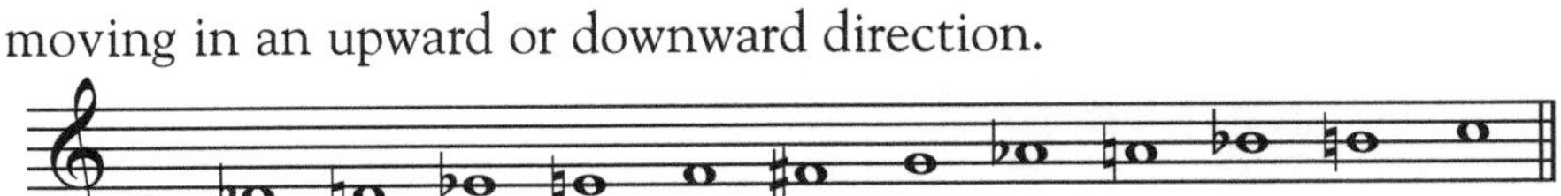

Play a chromatic scale on a keyboard. Starting on middle C, play every white and black key in order until you reach the next C.

BONUS QUESTION

What are *tetrachords* and where did they originate?____

METHODS • 8

ACCIDENTALS

Name ____

What is that sign in music that looks like a tic-tac-toe game board and what does it do? Actually, that sign is an **accidental** called a **sharp**, which is a music symbol used to raise a pitch one half step. You are probably familiar with accidentals already. Here is a complete listing.

Name	Symbol	Function
Flat	♭	lowers the pitch half step
Double Flat	𝄫	lowers the pitch a whole step
Natural Sign	♮	cancels a prior accidental
Sharp	♯	raises the pitch half step
Double Sharp	𝄪	raises the pitch a whole step

These symbols for accidentals are placed right before the notehead to change that particular pitch. An accidental that is not part of the key signature is cancelled at the next barline.

SHARPS

Identify the following sharps by placing their names in the blanks below these notes. Then find the notes on the keyboard below and label the key with the name of the note.

Ex.

________ ________ ________

FLATS

Identify the following flats by placing their names in the blanks below these notes. Then find the notes on the keyboard below and label the key with the name of the note.

Ex.

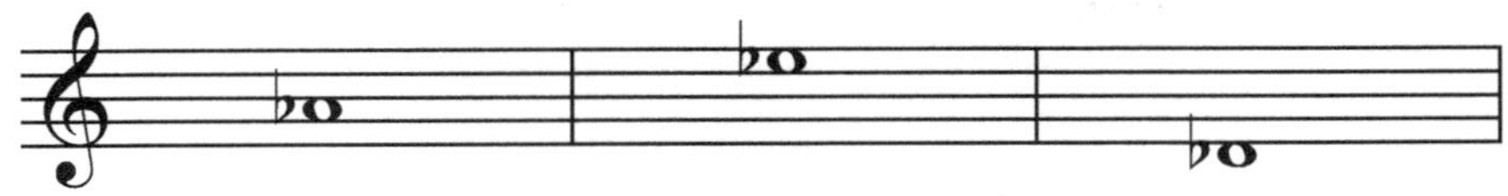

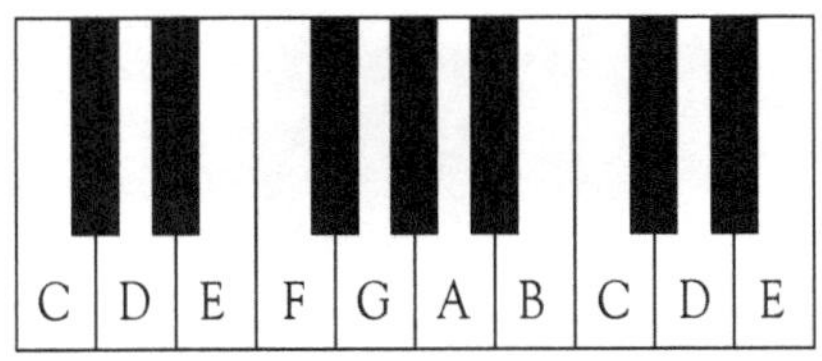

WHAT IS WRONG HERE?

To show you how necessary accidentals are in the music, have these melodies played exactly as written as you follow the notes carefully. Circle the note in each example that does not sound right. Does that note need to be raised (with a sharp) or lowered (with a flat) to make the melody correct?

The name **enharmonic** tone is given to notes that can be written as either sharps or flats. For example, C♯ is the same as D♭ as shown below. Now label the notes in the second example with their enharmonic names.

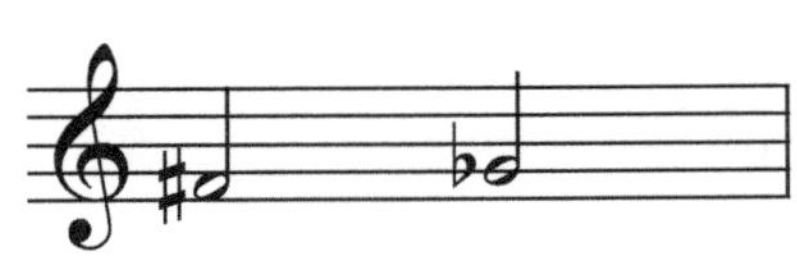

BONUS QUESTIONS

1. Is there such a thing as E sharp? What other name would that note have? ____________________

____

2. Can there be a C flat? What other name would that note have? ____________________

____

METHODS • 9

INTERVALS

Name ______________________________

An important component in the study of melody is the concept of **intervals**, or the distance in pitch between two notes. As far back in history as the 6th century B.C., a philosopher named Pythagoras believed that the ratio of musical intervals corresponded to the dimensions of the planets.

MELODIC • HARMONIC

Moving from one single note to the next in a melody, either lower or higher, creates a **melodic interval**. If notes are performed together, we hear a **harmonic interval**.

Melodic Intervals

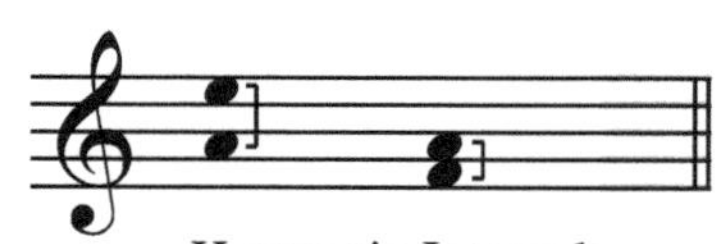

Harmonic Intervals

Look at the melodic intervals below. Sing or play each one. Can you think of a song that uses each of these intervals? Note how the interval from low C to high C is called an **octave** instead of an eighth. You will learn more about octaves below.

Second Third Fourth Fifth Sixth Seventh Octave

On the staff below, you see harmonic intervals. Have each one played. Which harmonic intervals sound the most pleasing to you?

Second Third Fourth Fifth Sixth Seventh Octave

OCTAVES

Since we know that only seven letters of the alphabet are used in music (A B C D E F G), in order to play a scale of eight notes, you will start over when reaching the eighth pitch, ending on the same letter name you started with, only an octave higher (or lower).

C D E F G A B C

The interval formed by playing the lower C and skipping to the upper C is called an **octave,** coming from a Latin word meaning "eight" and is a distance of eight notes apart. Play a lower level pitch on a piano or barred instrument, then play the same pitch an octave above (A to A or F to F, etc.) Describe the differences in the two sounds and also how they are alike.

Intervals that are smaller than an octave (eight note span) are called **simple intervals**, but those larger than an octave are called **compound intervals.**

INTERESTING INTERVALS

Now let's get some practice at identifying these intervals you have been reading about. In the examples below, give the intervals a numerical name such as third, fifth, etc. Notice that the first one is done for you. (If you need to, count lines and spaces from the lower pitch to the upper pitch until you can recognize them readily by sight.) Tell if they are melodic intervals or harmonic intervals by placing M or H below each line.

Ex.

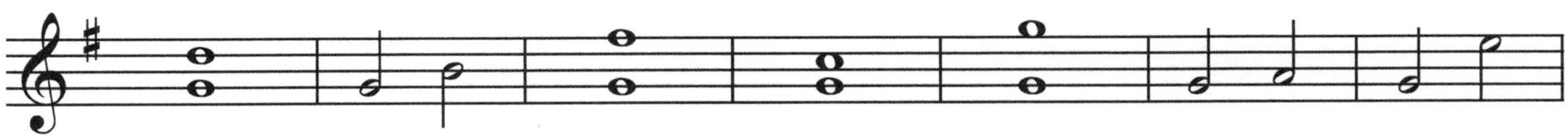

fifth ______ ______ ______ ______ ______ ______

H

On these examples, use the note given as your lower note and add a note to construct the interval requested under the example. The first one is done for you.

Ex.

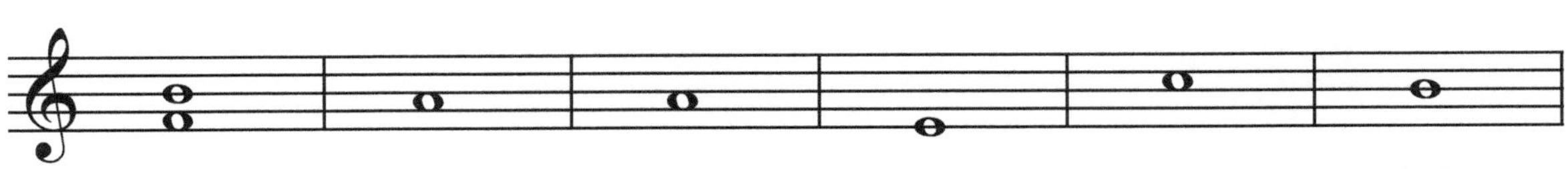

fourth seventh third second fifth sixth

BONUS QUESTIONS

1. What interval is made from the second to the third notes of "Twinkle, Twinkle, Little Star"?

____

2. What interval is heard on the first two notes of "I've Been Working on the Railroad"?

____

3. What interval occurs on the first two notes of the song "My Bonnie Lies Over the Ocean"?

____

4. What interval is made from the first two notes of "Oh, When the Saints Go Marching In"?

____

METHODS • TEST 10

MELODIC MASTERY TEST

Name ______________________________

In the first nine lessons, you have learned about **phrases**, **contour**, **rhythm**, **scales**, **accidentals** and **intervals**. Use this review to test yourself about how much you remember about melody before we move on.

1. Write your own definitions of these terms relating to melody:

accidental ______________________________

interval ______________________________

octave ______________________________

phrase ______________________________

2. Label these examples as conjunct or disjunct melodies:

____

____

3. Draw the curved phrase lines over the staff on the example below:

4. Write in the rhythm syllables (ta, ti, or ti-ti) under this example of notation:

5. Explain what each number tells in this time signature:

3 = ______________________________

4 = ______________________________

6. Write the symbol for Common Time and tell what time signature it represents.

(symbol)______________ = (time signature) ____________

7. Write the symbol for Cut Time and tell what time signature it represents.

(symbol) ________________ = (time signature) ______________

8. Name the three types of meter.

_________________, _________________, and _____________________.

9. Write the seven alphabet letters used in music to name pitches:

______ ______ ______ ______ ______ ______ ______

10. Write the letters used in a C Major scale in order:

______ ______ ______ ______ ______ ______ ______ ______

11. Name three kinds of minor scales.

_________________, _________________ and ______________________.

12. Which numbered notes are missing in a pentatonic scale.

_________ and _________

13. Draw and name the five possible accidentals in these boxes:

_______ _______ _______ _______ _______

14. In your own words, describe a motive.______________________________________

____

15. Give a numerical name to each of these intervals:

________ ________ ________ ________

SOLFÈGE

Name ______________________________

SOLFÈGE

To make hearing and singing melodic intervals easier, some people use the system of solfège. This system assigns syllables to each note of a scale. Perhaps you are familiar with these syllables. Sing the following C major scale using solfège syllables.

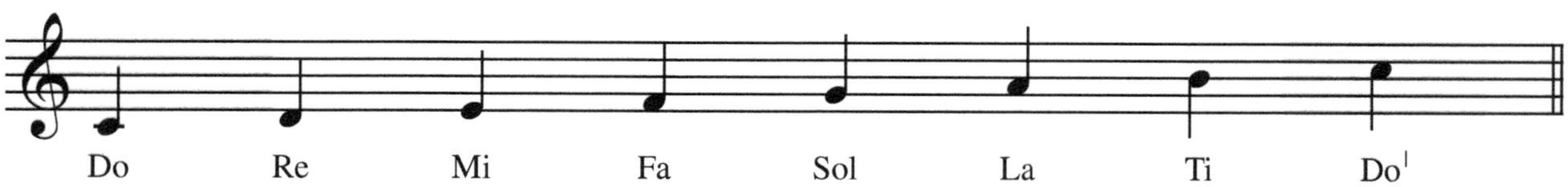

PROGRESSION

The easiest and earliest songs that we learned probably used the interval of a descending minor third. Think of yelling to a friend across the playground. How would you yell, "John-ny"? The interval of a minor third uses the syllables Sol, Mi. Here is an example of a Sol-Mi song.

1. Clap and count the rhythm of the Sol-Mi song excerpt above.
2. Next sing using the solfège syllables instead of the text.
3. Finally, sing with the words of the song.

Next, let's add the pitch on the syllable La. Here is an example of a Sol-Mi-La song

Circle the pitch La in this song, then follow the same three steps as above with this song using Sol, La and Mi.

Now we'll add the syllables Do and Re to Sol, La and Mi, creating a pentatonic scale, which does not use the syllables Fa and Ti (the 4th and 7th notes of the scale).

Ex.

Label each note above with a solfège syllable. The first one is done for you.

Lastly, the syllables Fa and Ti are added to this progression of solfège reading. Remember in a major scale, the half steps fall between the 3rd and 4th pitches (Mi, Fa) and the 7th and 8th pitches (Ti, Do). Sing the C major scale on the previous page once more carefully noting where the half steps fall. Sing it going upward and also going downward.

HAND SIGNS

Do **Re** **Mi** **Fa** **Sol** **La** **Ti** **Do'**

To strengthen the use of syllables to read music notation, John Curwen created a hand sign for each syllable. These hand signs are still used as reinforcement for reading music.

Practice making these hand signs as you sing a major scale. Try using both hands with fingers facing, then with only one hand to see which you prefer.

Try singing the scale syllables again trampoline style with hand-signs:

Do-Re Do-Mi Do-Fa Do-Sol Do-La Do-Ti Do-Do'

Sing the scale syllables in reverse (bungee-jumping style) with hand signs:

Do'-Ti Do'-La Do'-Sol Do'-Fa Do'-Mi Do'-Re Do'-Do

BONUS QUESTION

1. What syllable name is given to the half step between Fa and Sol? _____ between Sol and La? _____ and between La and Ti _____?
2. What syllables make up an arpeggio, starting on low Do? ____________________

MATERIALS • 11

12

FLASHCARDS

Name ______________________________

Becoming familiar with solfège syllables and hand signs will speed up your ability to read and sing music. To practice using solfège syllables, make flashcards, for use both individually and as a class. You are encouraged to make a small set of solfège flashcards (3 x 5) for your personal use and another large set (8 1/2 x 11) for class activities. The cards below have been abbreviated by using only the first letter of each syllable. You may choose to use the entire syllable on your cards.

LEVEL ONE

Suggestions for Using Flashcard Sets One and Two (treble clef):

1. Make note of which solfège syllables are included in Sets One and Two and which are omitted.
2. Practice singing the patterns on your own using hand signs. Notice that high Do' is set apart from low Do with an identifying mark (D').
3. Have a leader hold up one card at a time for the class to sing.
4. Divide into teams within the class for a contest with a winning team that can sing the most cards correctly.
5. Read four cards across from left to right for longer patterns.

FLASHCARDS: SET ONE		FLASHCARDS: SET TWO	
D M D S	M S D M	S L S M	L S S L
D M S D	M S M D	S L S L	L S L S
D S M S	M S S D	S M S M	L S L L
D M M S	M S S M	S L M M	L L S S
D R M S	M R D S	S M L S	L D' S L
D R D S	M D M S	S L L S	L L S D'
D M R M	M D M D	S S L S	D' S L S
D R D R	M S D S	S L M S	L S L D'
D S M D	M R D M	S M L L	D' L S S
D M S M	M R M D	S L S S	D' L L S

LEVEL TWO

Suggestions for Using Flashcard Sets Three and Four (treble clef):

1. Star the cards in each set that start on low DO, and then label the starting syllable for cards in each set.
2. Sing the first column in Set Three as a canon with half the class starting one card earlier than the other half.
3. Sing each column using hand signs.
4. Figure out the letter names of notes on each card, making note of accidentals in key signatures.
5. Play the pitches found on each card on a keyboard or barred instrument.

FLASHCARDS: SET THREE

(sol-mi) *(sol-mi-la)*

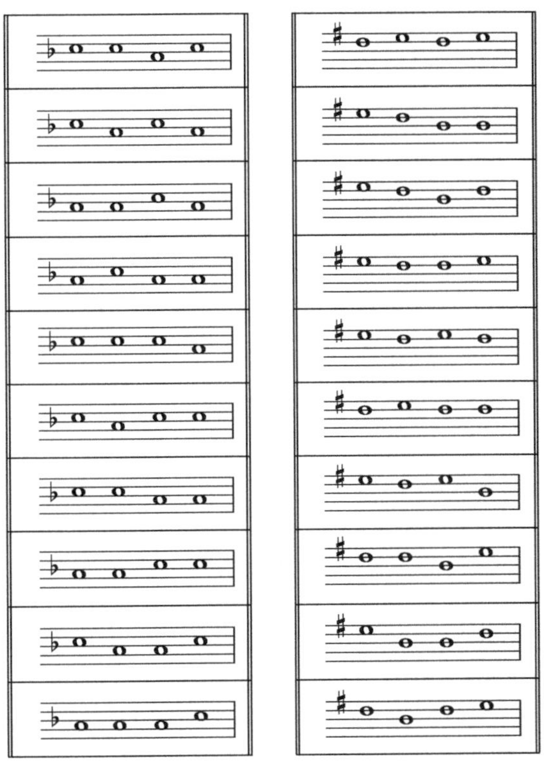

FLASHCARDS: SET FOUR

(la-sol-mi-re-do) *(do-la-sol-mi-re-do)*

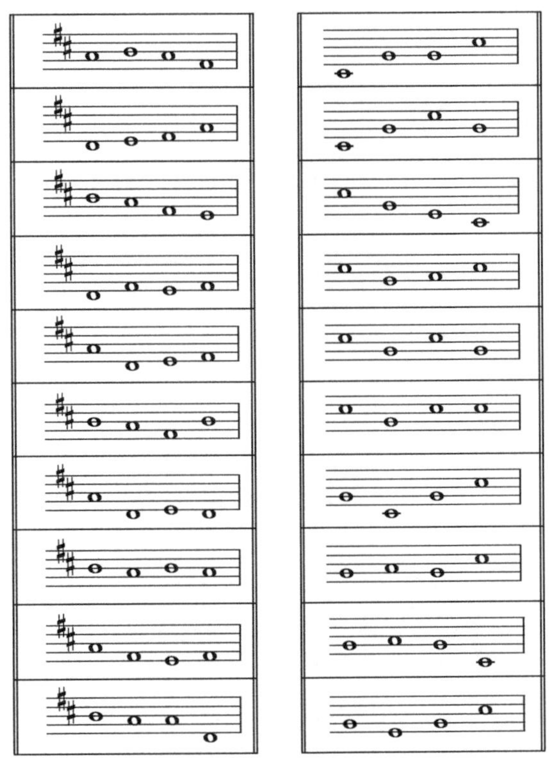

BONUS QUESTIONS

1. What is the scale called when Fa and Ti are omitted? ______________________________
2. Put a syllable letter (D, R, M, S, or L) under each note in this rhythm phrase, then practice and sing what you have written.

MATERIALS • 12

13

KEY SIGNATURES

Name ______________________________

Now that you've learned about scale patterns, it is time to discover how accidentals play a part in the formation of key signatures. Basically, the appearance of these sharps or flats at the beginning of a piece indicates that those particular notes are to raised (♯) or lowered (♭) throughout that piece.

In printed music, the necessary sharps and flats (one or the other) are found at the start of each line of music, following the clef sign, making up the key signature.

KEY OF C MAJOR

The key of C major has no sharps or flats and looks like this:

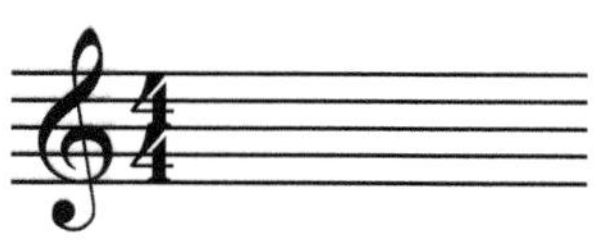

SHARPS

There are seven key signatures that use sharps:

Key of G – one sharp (F♯)
Key of D – two sharps (F♯ and C♯)
Key of A – three sharps (F♯, C♯ and G♯)
Key of E – four sharps (F♯, C♯, G♯ and D♯)
Key of B – five sharps (F♯, C♯, G♯, D♯ and A♯)
Key of F♯ – six sharps (F♯, C♯, G♯, D♯, A♯ and E♯)
Key of C♯ – seven sharps (F♯, C♯, G♯, D♯, A♯, E♯ and B♯)

The order of sharps from left to right in a key signature is always F♯, C♯, G♯, D♯, A♯, E♯ and B♯, a good thing to know. The sharp sign is placed on the line or space of the note it alters. For example, the F♯ is placed on the first space or fifth line.

Using the chart above, label the key signatures below:

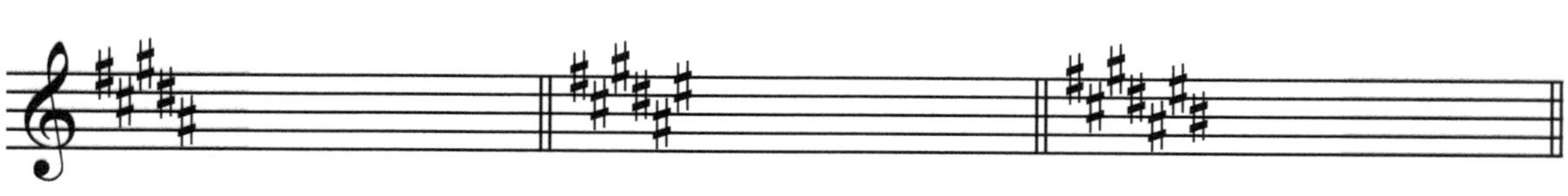

You can always tell what key you are in using sharps, by going up a half step from the last sharp in the signature.

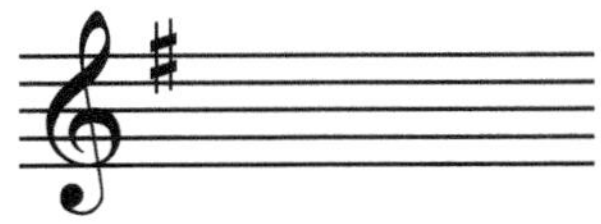

When you go a half step up from F♯, you know you are in the key of G.

FLATS

There are seven key signatures that use flats:

Key of F – one flat (B♭)
Key of B♭ - two flats (B♭ and E♭)
Key of E♭ - three flats (B♭, E♭ and A♭)
Key of A♭ - four flats (B♭, E♭, A♭ and D♭)
Key of D♭ - five flats (B♭, E♭, A♭, D♭ and G♭)
Key of G♭ - six flats (B♭, E♭, A♭, D♭, G♭ and C♭)
Key of C♭ - seven flats (B♭, E♭, A♭, D♭, G♭, C♭ and F♭)

The order of flats from left to right in a key signature is always B♭, E♭, A♭, D♭, G♭, C♭ and F♭, a good thing to remember. The flat sign is placed on the line or space of the note it alters. For example, the B♭ is placed on the third line.

Using the chart above, label the key signatures below:

______ ______ ______ ______

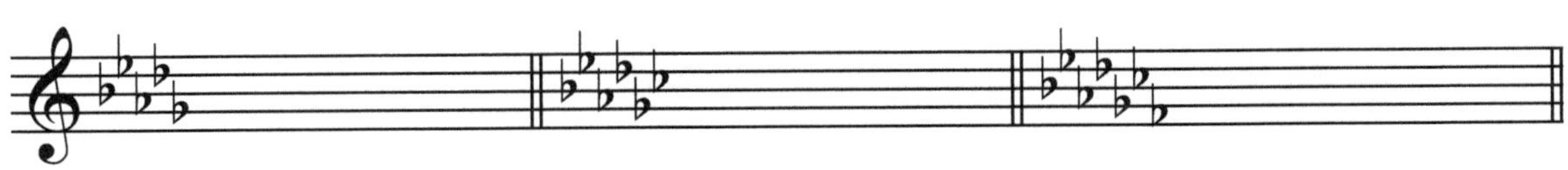

______ ______ ______

To find which key you are in using flats, go backwards one flat in the signature from the last flat added.

With three flats (B♭, E♭ and A♭) go back one flat from the last flat (A♭) to know that you are in the key of E♭. (You will simply need to memorize the key of F, which only has one flat.)

BONUS QUESTIONS:

1. Is a natural sign (♮) ever used in key signatures? ________ What is its purpose?

____

2. What other name is given the note B♯? _____ C♭? _____ E♯? _______

MATERIALS • 13

14

CIRCLE OF FIFTHS

Name ____

Most serious musicians memorize all the key signatures, but some find it easier to learn them using a diagram called the **Circle of Fifths**. The circle gives the appearance of a clock face and the word "fifths" is used because each new key starts on the fifth scale degree of the key before it, as you will see.

Make your own Circle of Fifths below using the diagram provided. We have started it for you by entering the key of C in the top square and putting 0 in the circle below it, meaning that the key of C has no sharps or flats. Then start down the right side for sharps putting the name of the next key in the square and the number of sharps in the small circle.

When finished, start down the left side for flats, putting the name of the next key in the box and the number of flats in the small circle.

When you get to the three circles at the bottom, you will be putting both sharps and flats in each one, with sharps on top and flats on the bottom.

CIRCLE OF FIFTHS

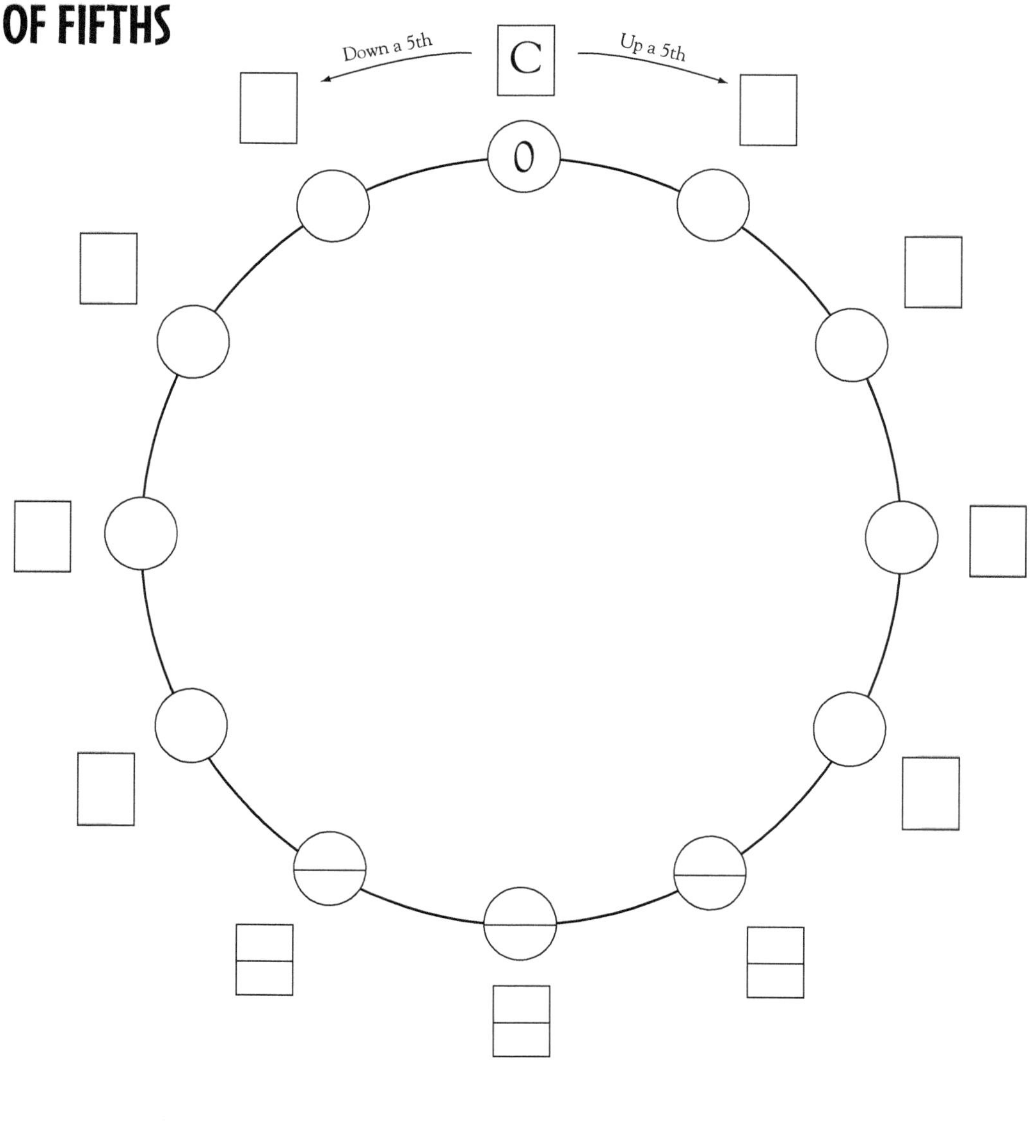

Note the three keys at the bottom of the circle will have different key signatures but will sound the same as the other key in the box. That's because they are **enharmonic**, which means the same notes are played but just "spelled" differently. For example, C♯ is the same note as D♭, F♯ is the same note as G♭ and B is the same note as C♭. If these major keys were played, they would sound just the same, played on the exact same notes.

MAJOR VS. RELATIVE MINOR

You learned the major and minor scales in the lesson on scales. Each major key shares a key signature with a minor key. That minor key is said to be the **relative minor** (performed as a natural minor scale) of the major key. For example, the key of C has no sharps and flats; the key of A minor also has no sharps and flats. A minor is the relative minor of C major. You can always find the relative minor by going a minor third down from the tonic or key tone of the major scale.

Fill in the blanks below to name the relative minor of the major key. Write the name of the minor keys in lower case. The first one is done for you.

1. Key of C major has a relative minor of __a__ (minor third down from C)
2. Key of F major has a relative minor of _____.
3. Key of D major has a relative minor of _____.
4. Key of A major has a relative minor of _____.

WHO HAS THE KEYS?

Under the following examples, write the name of the major key signature and its relative minor.

a.

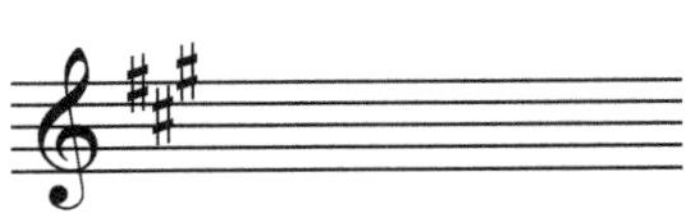

Major minor

b.

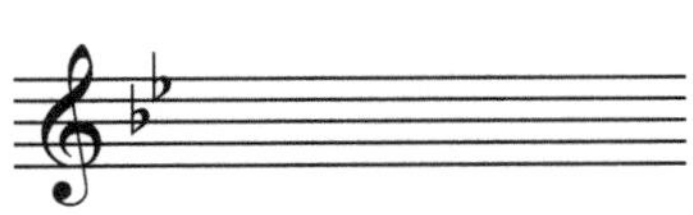

Major minor

c.

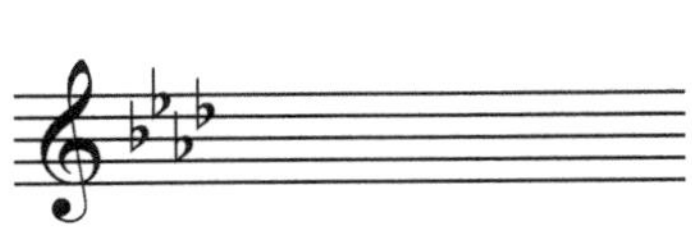

Major minor

d.

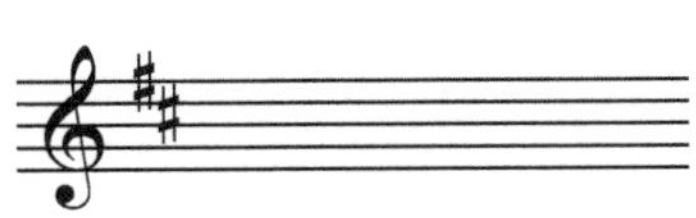

Major minor

BONUS QUESTIONS:

1. How many flats are in the key of E♭? _____ Name those flats __________________

2. How many sharps are in the key of F♯? _____ Name those sharps ________________

GRAND STAFF/LEDGER LINES

Name ______________________________

It is difficult to imagine how all the music of the world from ages past to the present has been created using pitches named from only seven letters of the alphabet (A B C D E F and G). As music is notated, each of these seven pitch names is given a particular place of significance on the staff, which is made up of five horizontal lines with four spaces in between.

Staff

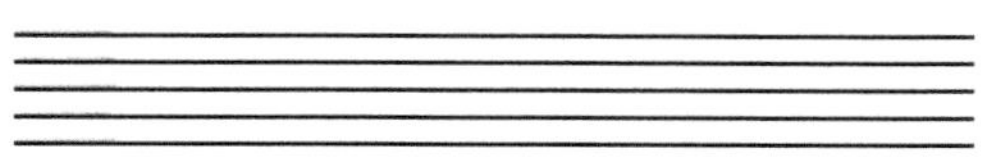

Each line and space is given a number name, starting from the bottom to the top.

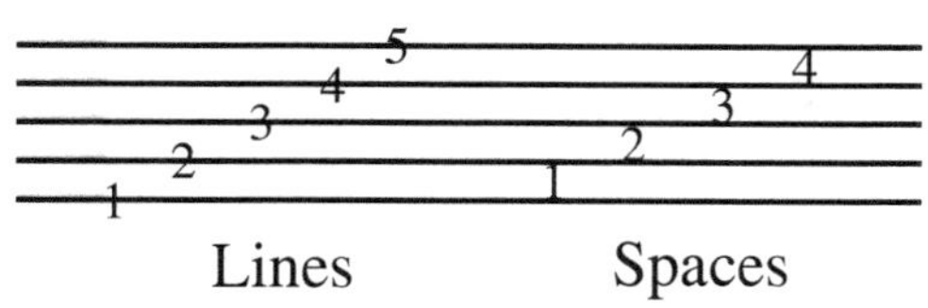

Each line and space is also given a letter name and it is important to note at this point that there are two sets of lines and spaces, one indicating the treble clef (centered around G) and another for the bass clef (centered around F). When playing piano music, the right hand plays the notes placed on the treble clef staff while the left hand plays the notes on the lower bass clef staff.

Treble Clef:

Bass Clef:

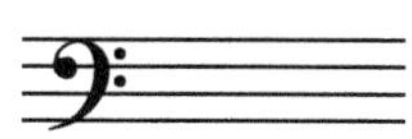

As you can see when the upper staff is joined to the bottom clef, the result is known as the **grand staff** as shown here:

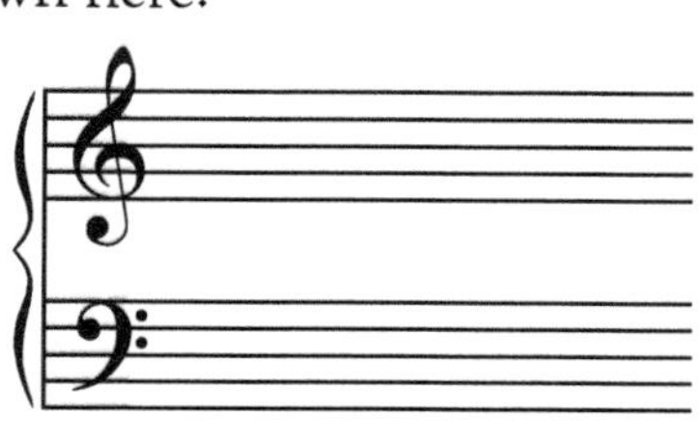

Grand Staff

PRACTICE MAKES PERFECT

Practice making each of the clef signs, following these examples. First by connecting the dots, then make one on your own in the square provided.

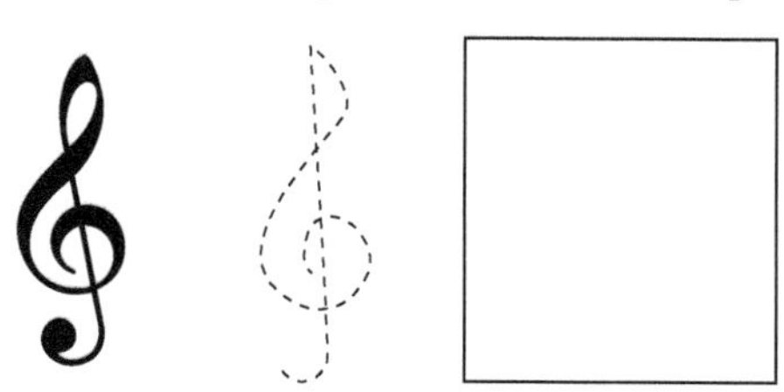

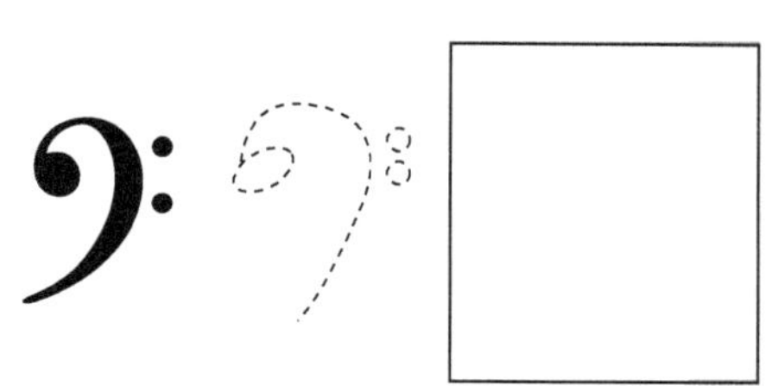

LEDGER LINES

You must have wondered how only seven letters could be used over and over on a staff and continue to ascend higher or go lower. The solution is the use of extra lines called **ledger lines**, which go above, below and in between the staves. These extensions give only enough room to write one note on each ledger line but make music easier to read.

(Treble Clef)

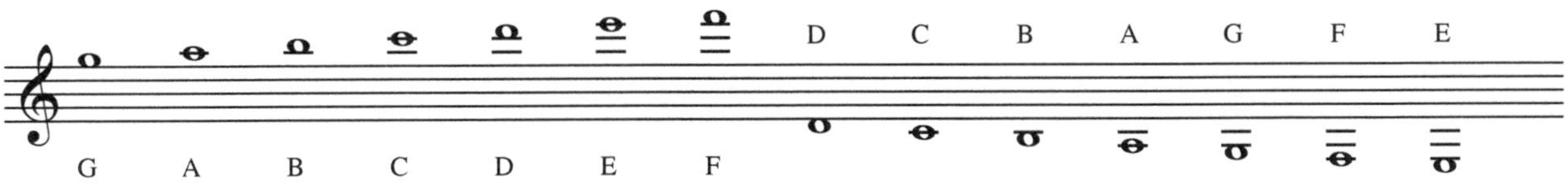

(Bass Clef)

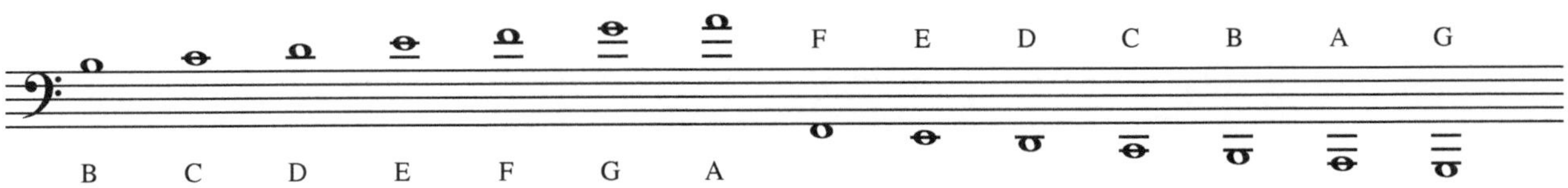

SPELL WORDS

Write the letter names below each of the notes to form a word. Use the chart above for the notes on ledger lines. The notes on the staff you should already know. Note which clef you are working in since the names of the lines and spaces are different in each clef.

a. 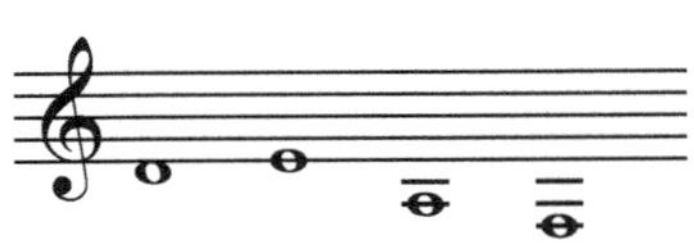

____

b. 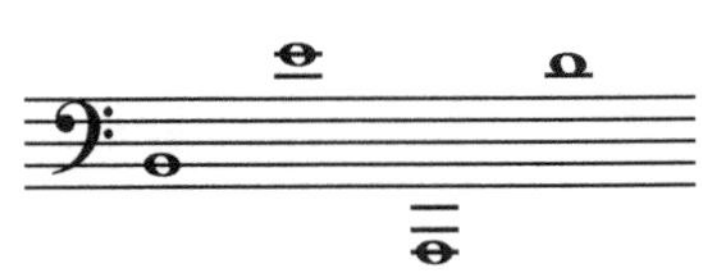

____

c. 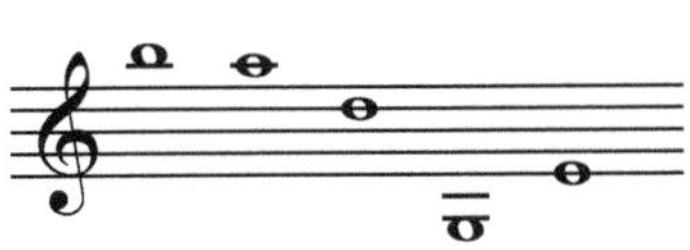

____

d. 

____

BONUS ACTIVITY:

Put notes on the staff to spell a word of your choice, one for treble clef and one for bass clef. Use ledger lines if you can.

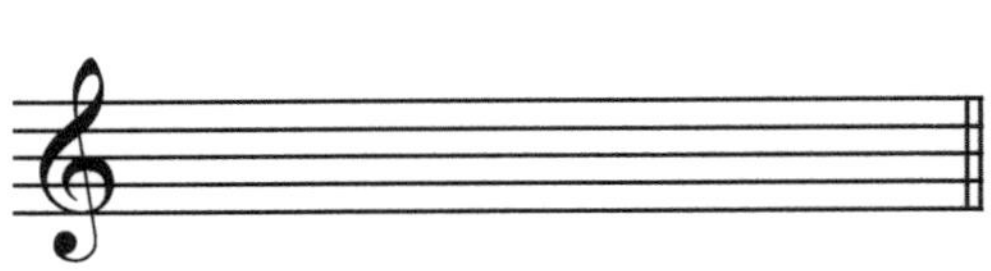

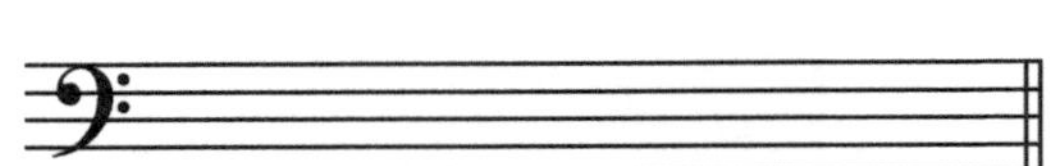

MATERIALS • 15

16

NOTATION

Name ______________________________

Even though there is evidence of music being used centuries ago, there was no known system for notating music until the 12th century. Musicians then began to use letters to give names to pitches. Composers were notating music almost as it is today by the 17th century, meaning that it took over 500 years to create a way to write music on a staff that is recognized universally today.

From the 9th century and later, the symbols that became notes were called *neumes* (pronounced "nooms") or *neumatic notation*. At first, these generic symbols were used on a four line staff without bar lines to show direction, not exact pitch or rhythm duration.

Ex.

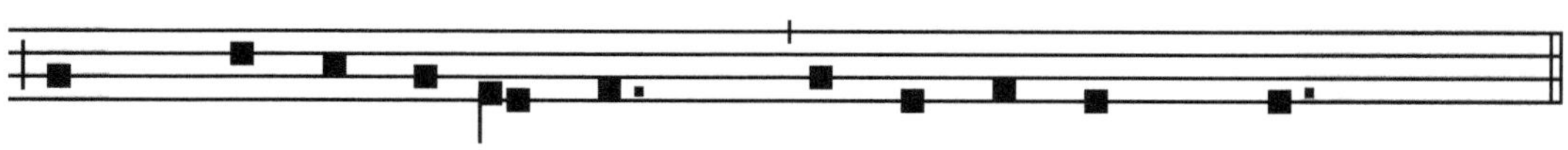

REVIEW THE BASICS

Remember the two clef signs that are used at the beginning of each staff? Label each staff with the correct name:

Ex.

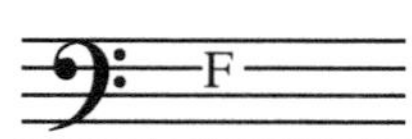

____________ ____________

When two staves are joined together, the result is shown below. Give the correct name for this staff:

Ex.

____________ ____________

In the early years, notation was hand printed and was used to help the musician memorize the music to be performed, giving clues that only the performer could need. Later the notation not only showed exact pitches and rhythm, but also gave hints about what the composer had in mind when the piece was written.

In this example of printed music, show what you have learned in previous lessons by filling in the blanks with the following information as requested:

- Rhythm syllables: ta, ti, ta-a
- Solfège syllables: Do, Re, Mi, Fa, Sol, La, Ti, Do'
- Kind of note: Q = quarter note, E = eighth note, H = half note, DH = dotted half note
- Letter names of notes: A, B, C, D, E, F, G

Ex. (Line 1)

Rhythm ___ ___ ___ ___ ___ ___ ___ ___ ___ ___ ___ ___

Solfège ___ ___ ___ ___ ___ ___ ___ ___ ___ ___ ___ ___

Note kind ___ ___ ___ ___ ___ ___ ___ ___ ___ ___ ___ ___

Letter names ___ ___ ___ ___ ___ ___ ___ ___ ___ ___ ___ ___

Ex. (Line 2)

Rhythm ___ ___ ___ ___ ___ ___ ___ ___ ___ ___ ___ ___ ___ ___ ___

Solfège ___ ___ ___ ___ ___ ___ ___ ___ ___ ___ ___ ___ ___ ___ ___

Note kind ___ ___ ___ ___ ___ ___ ___ ___ ___ ___ ___ ___ ___ ___ ___

Letter names ___ ___ ___ ___ ___ ___ ___ ___ ___ ___ ___ ___ ___ ___ ___

BONUS QUESTION

1. Why are G clef and F clef appropriate, additional names for the clef signs?

G Clef? ____

F Clef? ____

MATERIALS • 16

17

PIANO KEYBOARD

Name ____

How many times have you had the opportunity to sit at a piano and pick out a familiar melody? Perhaps you even have a piano at home or an electronic keyboard, which is quite popular today as an alternative.

The **pianoforte** (as the piano was originally called) and the violin go back to the time of the classical composer, Ludwig van Beethoven. Invented in 1711 by an Italian named Bartolommeo Cristofori, the first piano was designed to reproduce the range of a full orchestra. It was called a *pianoforte* because it could play softly (*piano*) or loudly (*forte*), depending upon how hard the keys were struck.

Look inside a piano as it is played and you will discover how the sounds are made. A set of tuned strings of varying sizes are secured inside a case made of wood and struck by felt covered mallets when a key is played.

These keyboard instruments have survived and evolved from their early prototypes:

The **celesta** (meaning heavenly) is actually a percussion instrument invented by Mustel around 1880 and resembles a small upright piano. Instead of felt mallets hitting strings, hammers hit steel bars that produce high, bell-like tones. One can hear a celesta played in the "Dance of the Sugar Plum Fairy" from the *Nutcracker Suite* by Tchaikovsky.

The **harpsichord** was the most common stringed instrument of the 16th and 17th centuries and looks like a small grand piano. The strings are plucked by quills instead of being struck by hammers. Because of the mechanism, the volume does not vary, no matter how hard the keys are played.

The **organ** is an instrument whose origin can be traced back to Greece in the 4th century A. D., consisting of more than one keyboard and includes pedals for the feet to play. Mechanisms called stops are used to vary the sounds made by a registry of pipes through which air is pumped.

The **piano** is an instrument with separate (up to three) strings tuned in unison for each pitch and struck by felt mallets. Also a series of dampers is used so the sound won't be sustained longer than desired. Pianos are made in two shapes, the wing-shaped grand piano and the upright box-style, sometimes called a spinet.

A regular piano has eighty-eight keys ranging from low to high with middle C to divide the bass clef (lower pitches) from the treble clef (higher pitches). It should be kept in perfect tune (A440) for optimum enjoyment. The keys are divided into white and black in a certain pattern which groups the black keys into twos and threes.

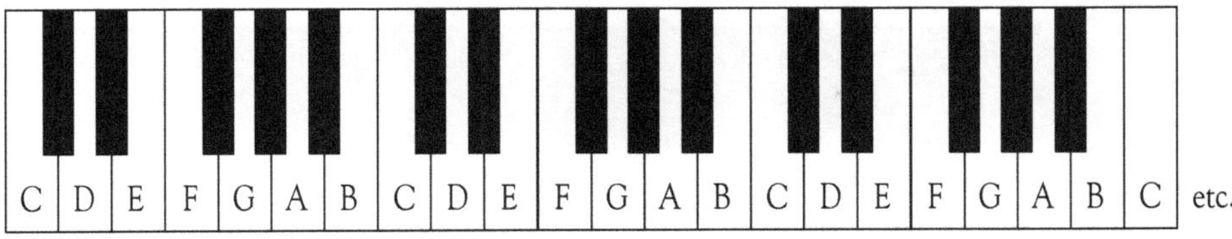

On the following example, put the names of the sharps over the black keys.

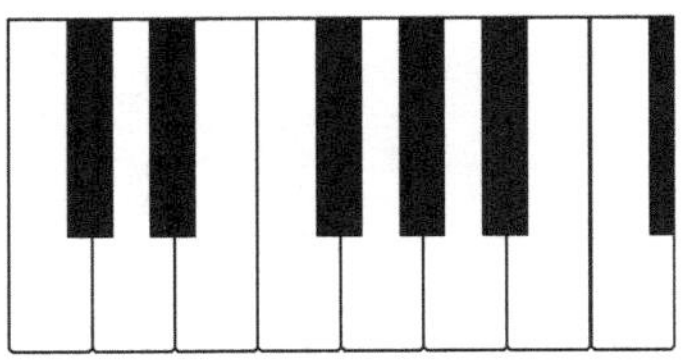

In this example, put the names of the flats over the black keys.

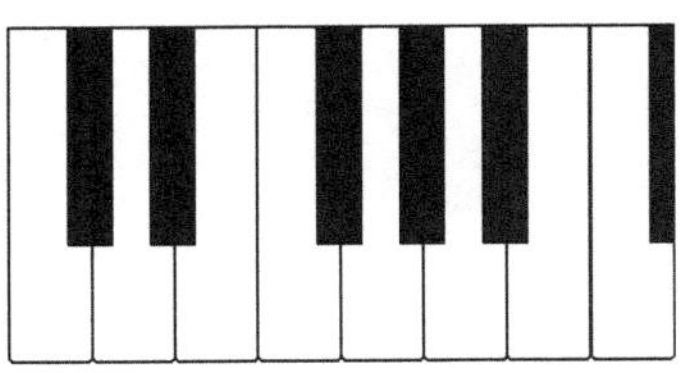

TRUE OR FALSE *(Put a T or F in the blank.)*

_____ 1. A *celesta* has felt mallets that hit strings.

_____ 2. The *harpsichord* cannot change volume when keys are played.

_____ 3. An *organ* has a row of pedals to be played with the feet.

_____ 4. The *piano* was first called a mezzoforte.

_____ 5. An *organ* has eighty-eight keys.

BONUS QUESTIONS

1. How does a harpsichord differ from a piano? ______________________________

____

2. How does an electronic synthesizer work? ______________________________

____

MATERIALS • 17

18

MELODY INSTRUMENTS

Name ______________________________

Even though the piano became the instrument of choice for homes and schools in the 19th century, other instruments are effective in the playing of melodies. For our purposes, we will take a closer look at barred Orff instruments, melody bells and then recorder (in Lesson 19).

ORFF INSTRUMENTS

A German teacher named Carl Orff (1895 – 1982) developed a method for teaching music to young children using instruments, movement, singing and rhythmic speech through improvisation. He opened a music school in 1924 and in 1936 presented thousands of children performing special dances at the opening of the Olympics.

Xylophones, metallophones and glockenspiels that make up the Orff instrumentarium have the capacity to not only play melodies, but also accompaniments for singing. These instruments come in various sizes labeled soprano, alto and bass, according to length of the bars.

Getting the best sound from these barred instruments depends on correct mallet technique:

1. Hold each mallet loosely with thumb, the first and second fingers about half way up the stem.
2. Palms should be downward with curved and flexible fingers.
3. Strike the center of the bar with the ball of the mallet, bouncing for maximum vibration.
4. Alternate hands in playing a melody or accompaniment.

To get some experience playing a barred instrument, set one up in a pentatonic scale (C, D, E, G and A), taking off the F and B bars for quicker recognition of bars and better accuracy. Have the teacher or a student leader say one phrase at a time of the rhyme below for instrumentalists to echo back in rhythm on any bars in the pentaton.

Acka backa soda cracker, (*echo*) Acka backa boo, (*echo*)

Acka backa soda cracker, (*echo*) Out goes you! (*echo*)

MELODY BELLS

For a change in tone color, use a set of melody bells to play simple melodies, individually or in small groups. Before students can accurately read music notation, melodies can be played on song bells using a number notation. Try the example below using E as #3, D as #2 and C as #1.

"Hot Cross Buns"

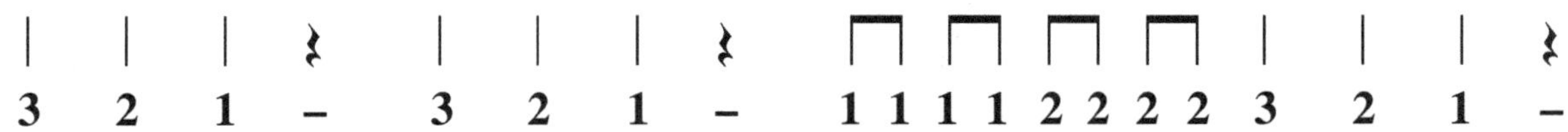

The first bell experiences are simplified by playing melodies in the key of C using only white keys with no accidentals. Melody bells can be used to play with a familiar melody being sung, reading only the letters.

"Frere Jacques"

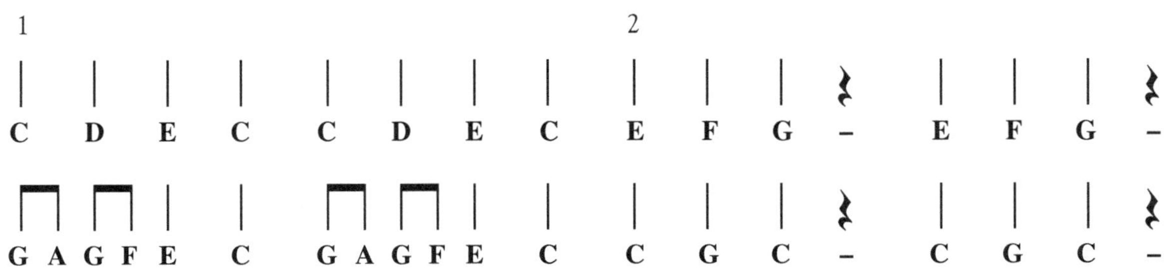

Practice playing and singing the song above using letter names, then play and sing the song as a round with a competent player leading each group. Group 1 starts. When group 1 gets to the number 2, then Group 2 starts at the beginning.

TRY SOMETHING DIFFERENT

For those who want to try an unusual musical project, here are some clever ideas to help you:

Tuned Bottles: Make an experiment out of tuning eight clean bottles to the Key of C as they are filled with varying amounts of water. You may tap the bottles to tune them using piano pitches as a guide, or blow into them to get a pitch. When your scale is set, cap the bottles to keep the pitches constant until ready for use.

Tuned Glasses: Try the same experiment above using stemmed drinking glasses. When the glasses are tuned, wet your index finger and rub along the rim for a ringing sound that can be tuned according to the amount of water in each glass.

BONUS QUESTIONS:

1. Does adding water in a bottle raise or lower the pitch?________________________

2. What is the pitch of a tuning fork and for what purpose is it used? ____________________

____

____

MATERIALS • 18

19

RECORDERS

Name ____

The **recorder** has a valuable potential as a pre-band instrument because it is relatively easy to play and inexpensive to own. It is a small instrument made of wood or plastic, held vertically and played as breath is blown into a mouthpiece.

With a flute-like sound, the recorder has been used to play solo melodies and in ensembles for many centuries. The use of recorders in music classes continues to grow because the reading of rhythm notation and pitch names soon becomes necessary to make progress. You will most likely first learn how to play the smallest one (the soprano recorder), but larger sizes are also available when you are ready, called alto, tenor and bass recorders.

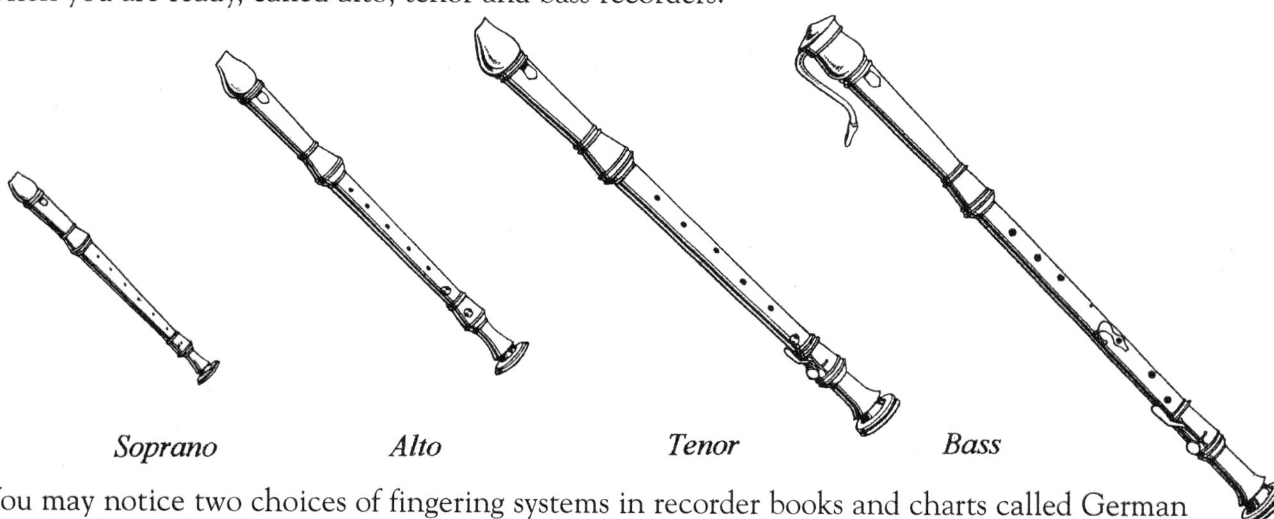

You may notice two choices of fingering systems in recorder books and charts called German and English or Baroque. The main difference on a soprano recorder is the playing and tuning of the F pitch. It is interesting to try both ways to play F to see if you can tell why two ways are suggested on this fingering chart.

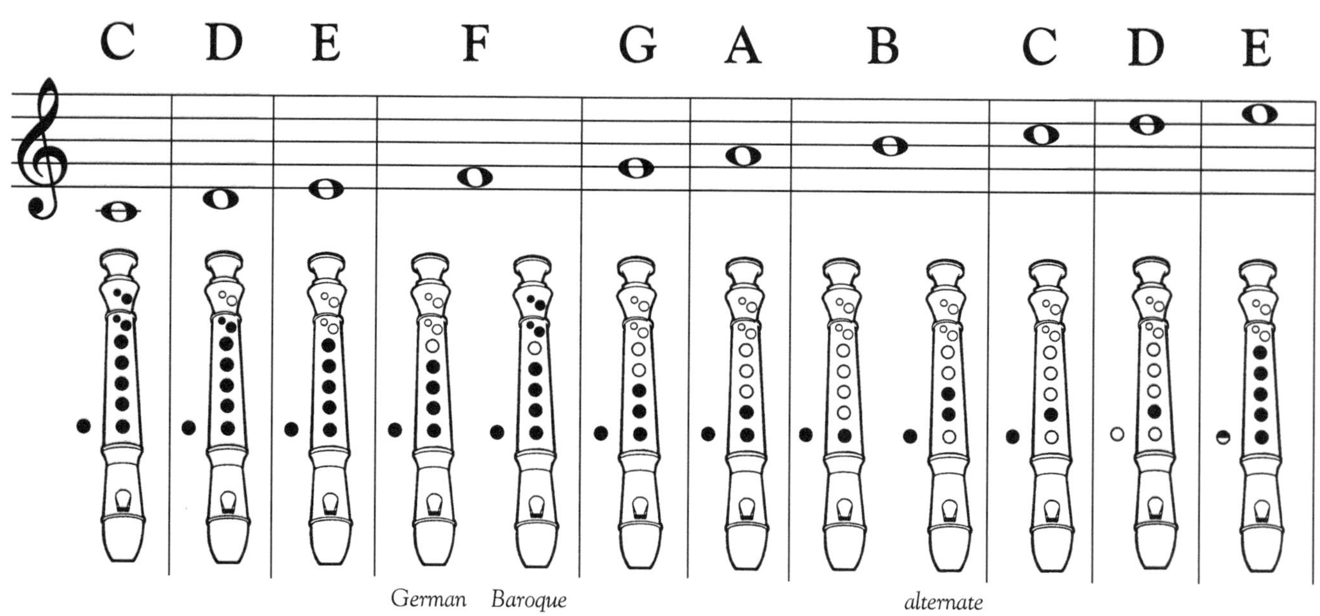

As you begin to play the recorder, get used to placing your left hand above the right hand, which may seem awkward at first. The left thumb will cover the hole on the back and first three fingers of the left hand will cover the top three holes of the recorder. The little finger of the left hand is never used. The fingers of the right hand will cover the lower holes as the right thumb is used to steady the instrument.

These three points will help you make a pleasant tone quickly as you start playing:

1. Sit up straight with arms at your sides, so the recorder is at a 45-degree angle.
2. Securely cover the holes with the soft pads of your fingers, not the tips.
3. Inhale through the mouth, and then blow softly, letting the tongue release the air, saying "Too."

IT'S IN THE B-A-G

All recorder methods suggest starting with the pitches B, A, and G, because only the left hand is required and control comes rather quickly. Review and label these three pitches on the staff, then play this example individually and as a class.

With the teacher or student volunteer as the leader, echo four-beat patterns using only B, A and G.

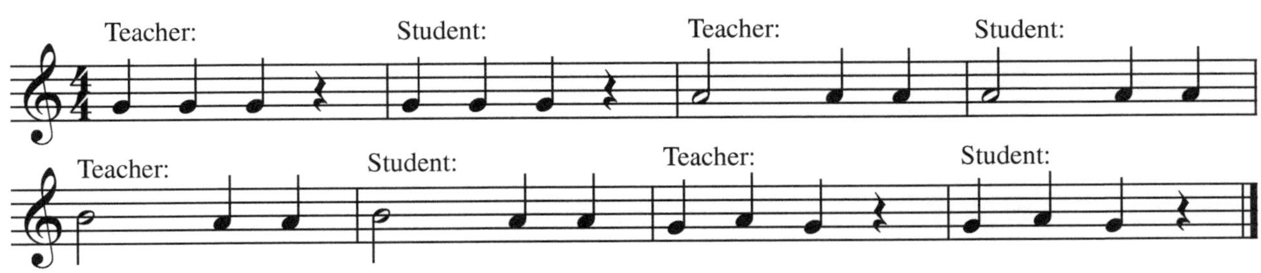

The next step is to read notation using B, A and G on your own. Here is the old favorite, "Hot Cross Buns" for you to play when you are ready to read the notes.

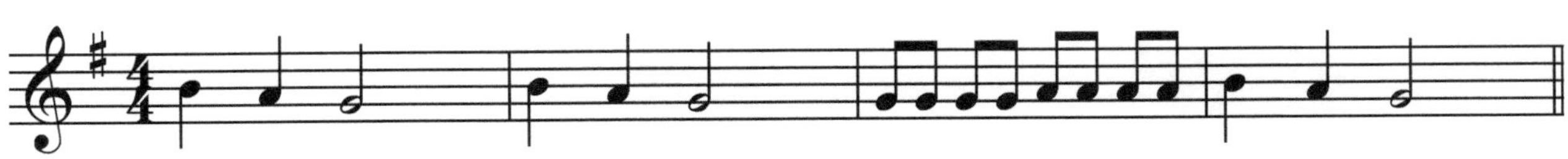

Get a recorder book to go on with your lessons and practice at home until you get a good musical sound and can play several melodies with skill.

BONUS QUESTIONS

1. Why is it necessary to have both German and English fingering systems?________________

____

2. Can you play this rhythmic example all on one pitch? Can you change pitches?

MATERIALS • TEST 20

MELODIC MASTERY TEST

Name ____

In the last nine lessons, you have learned about **solfège, hand signs, key signatures, the grand staff, notation, the piano keyboard** and **melodic instruments**. Follow the instructions below on each section to test your knowledge.

1. Match the hand signs by putting the letter of a picture in the blank of the corresponding solfège syllable:

________	1. Do	a.	
________	2. Re	b.	
________	3. Mi	c.	
________	4. Fa	d.	
________	5. Sol	e.	
________	6. La	f.	
________	7. Ti	g.	

2. Label these notes with the correct letter names to spell words:

a. 

___ ___ ___

b. 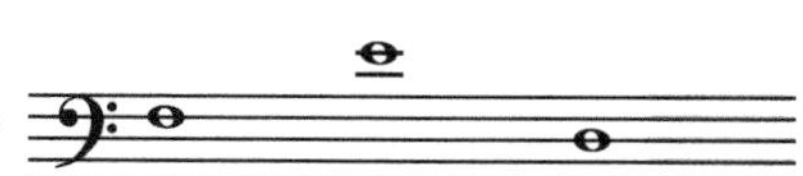

___ ___ ___

c. 

___ ___ ___ ___ ___

d. 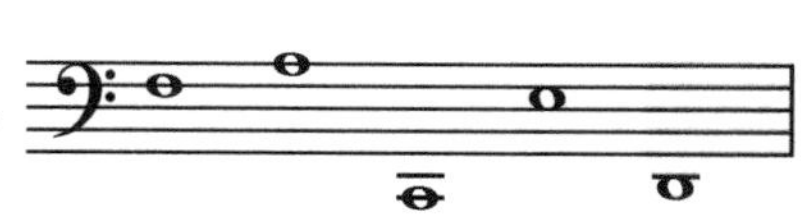

___ ___ ___ ___ ___

3. Name these major key signatures *(Bonus if you can name the relative minor of each one)*:

a.  ____________

b.  ____________

c. 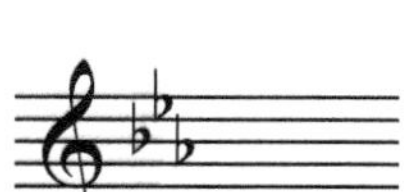 ____________

d.  ____________

4. Fill in the blanks:
   a. Complete the order of adding sharps; F♯, ______, G♯, ______, A♯, ______ and B♯.
   b. Complete the order of adding flats; B♭, ______, A♭, ______, G♭, ______ and F♭.
   c. Name the enharmonic note of G♯ ______ and B♭ ______
   d. Name the four most common sizes of recorders; ______________________, ______________________, ______________________ and ______________________.
   e. Which finger is never used to play a recorder? ______________________

5. Name the solfège syllables in the examples below, noting that Do is labeled for you:

a. 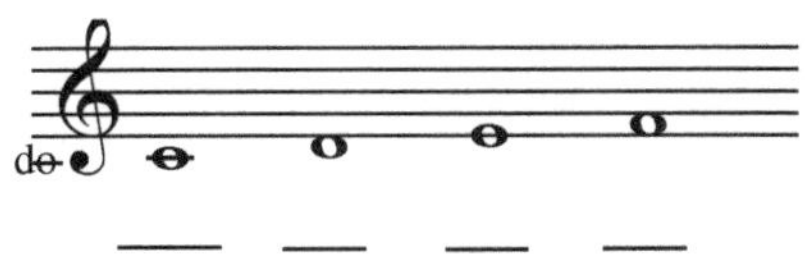

b. 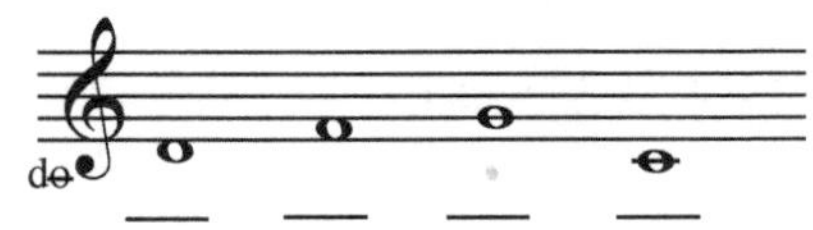

c. 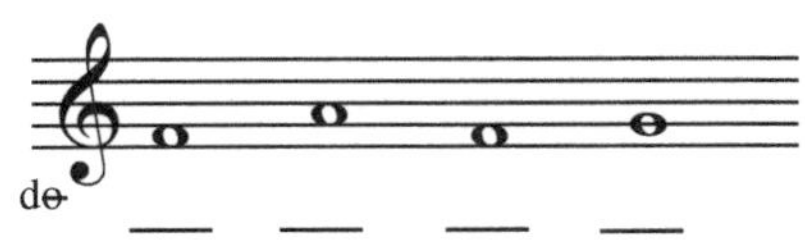

d. 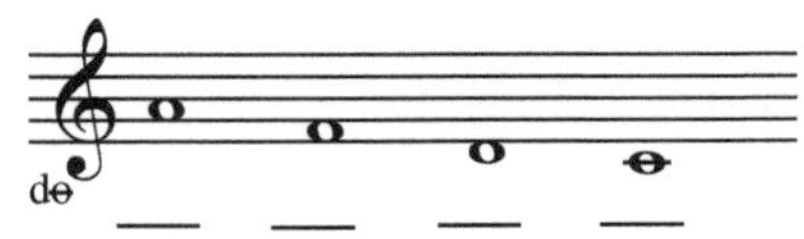

6. Match these syllables with the actual pitches by drawing a line to connect the pair:

a. 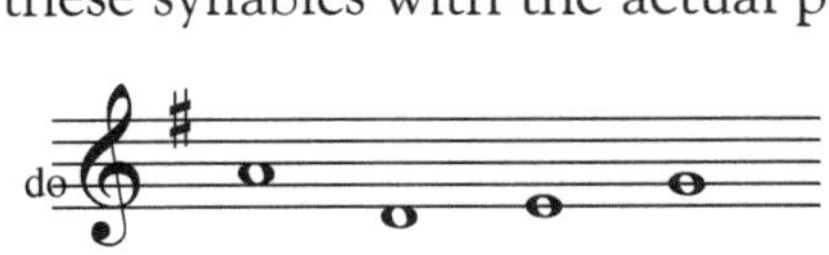

mi do re do

b. 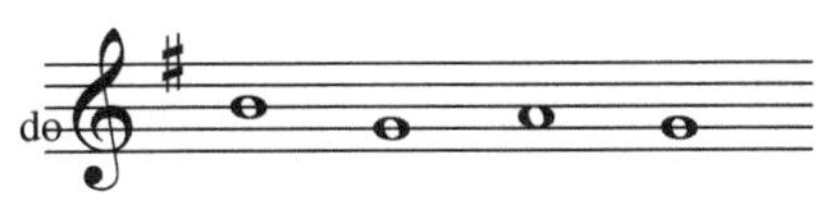

do re mi so

c. 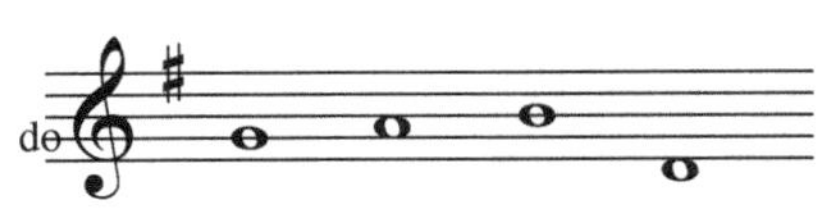

re so la do

7. Name these ledger lines in treble and bass clefs:

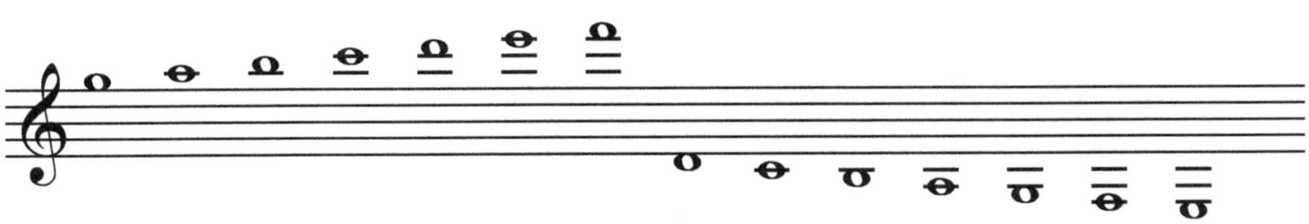

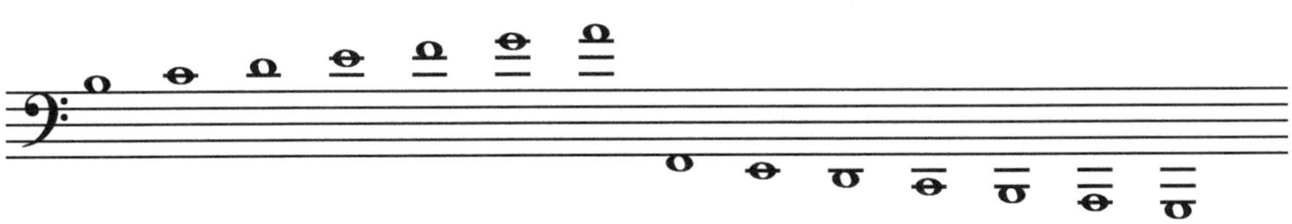

8. Label the keys of the piano keyboard with names of white keys on the bottom and black keys on the top. You may use sharps or flats for the black keys

MENTALITY • 19

21

SIGHT-READING

Name ______________________________

The term **sight-reading** refers to the skill of being able to perform a written musical composition without studying or rehearsing it first. To sight-read successfully, there must be an understanding of written pitches and rhythm symbols. In **sight-singing**, the musician should be able to sing a piece of music never seen before, demonstrating an ability to understand and perform the music symbols in the printed music.

GETTING READY

When sight-reading music, you must combine your knowledge of rhythm and melody. So far, you have had practice with each of these skills and should be ready to combine them, starting with simple examples.

1. Listen to a simple musical phrase on a keyboard. As you listen a second time, show the contour of the melody with hand levels in the air.
2. Draw a diagram of the melodic direction on paper, using a curved line, dashes or dots to connect.
3. Practice your rhythm by clapping these examples as you say the rhythm syllables:

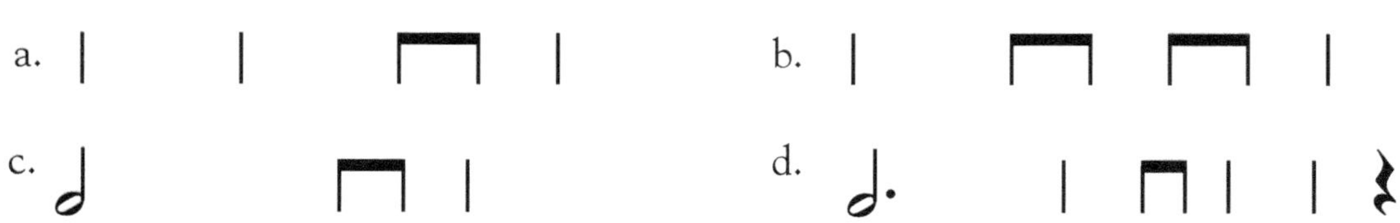

Read and sing these melodic patterns from a two line staff, using hand signs:

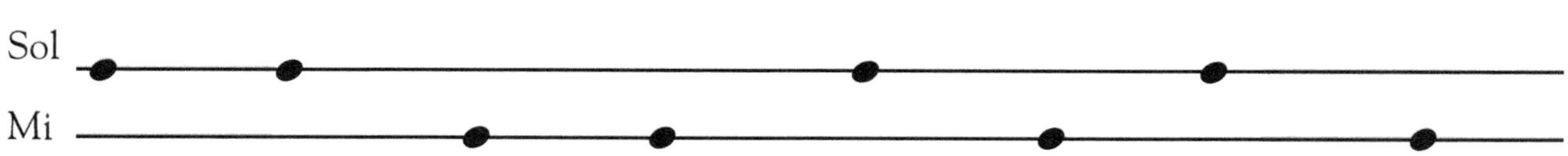

Read and sing these melodic patterns with rhythm added:

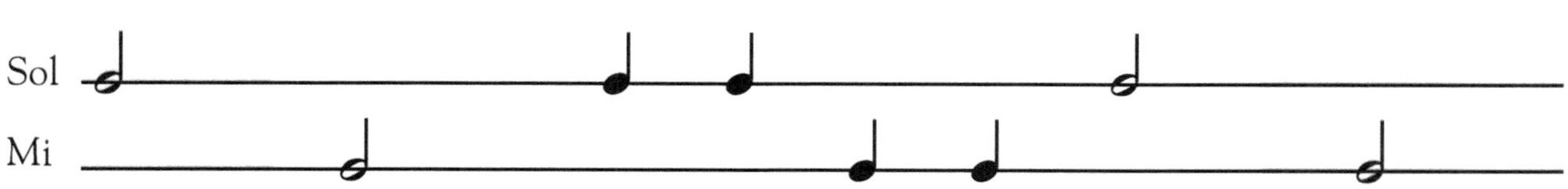

Add other solfège syllables to read, without the staff:

a. 

b. 

c. 

In the example below, label each note with a solfège syllable and rhythm syllable, then sing the excerpt using hand signs. The first note has been done for you. Can you identify the familiar song?

Song Title: ______________________________

Try your skills on another excerpt, labeling the solfège and rhythm syllables:

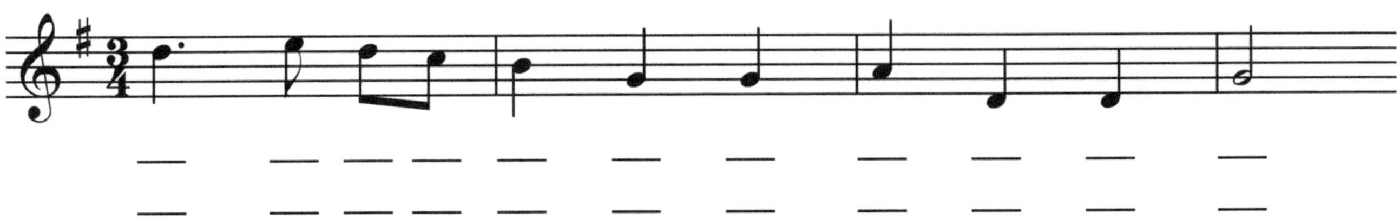

SIGHT-READING SEQUENCE

The more you sight-read, the easier it will become, using this four-step procedure:

1. Determine the time signature (how many beats per measure and which kind of note gets one beat).
2. Figure out the rhythm and practice clapping the patterns.
3. Discover the key signature and locate the tonic note or Do.
4. Sing each phrase, using solfège and hand signs (finding steps, skips and repeated notes).
5. Check your accuracy by playing the melody on an instrument.

BONUS QUESTIONS

1. What is meant by the term "playing by ear"? ______________________________

____

____

2. What is another name for the term "solfeggio"? ______________________________

HARMONY

Name ______________________________

Harmony refers to the concept of several tones being played or sung simultaneously or a combination of tones, adding interest and depth to a melodic line. Harmony was relatively unknown until the 9th century. Before then, only a single melodic line (horizontal element) was written down.

With the birth of harmony (vertical element) came the notion of playing or singing several tones at the same time. If a melody is all we ever hear of a composition, something of significant beauty is missing.

CHORDS

If three or more tones are performed together, the result is called a **chord** and the simplest chord to learn is the **triad**. As you might think, a triad is comprised of two intervals of a third and can be major or minor.

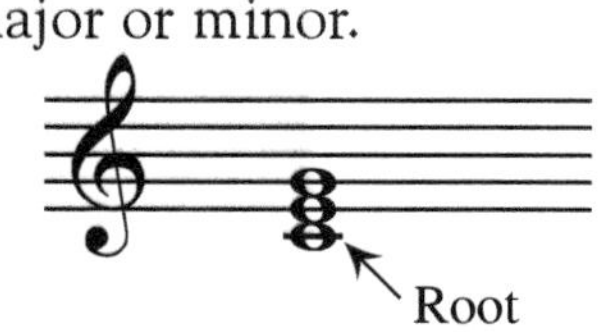

To build a triad chord, you start with a foundation or root note (Do or tonic, the first note of the scale), and then add a note a third above the root (Mi) and another note a third above the middle note (Sol).

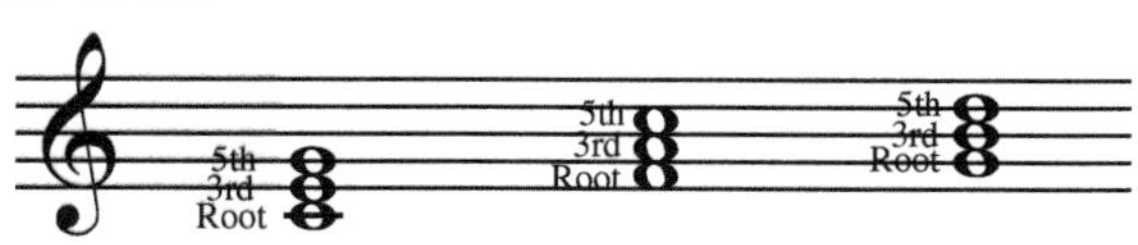

Practice building some tonic chords below, using the root note and key signature as guidelines for adding the two notes above. Play what you have written on a keyboard to check for accuracy.

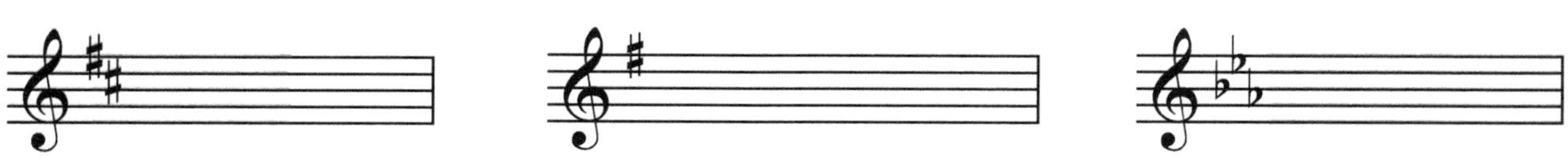

Other important chords in a key signature are those built on the fourth note of the scale, called **subdominant** and on the fifth note, called the **dominant**. Chords can also be identified by their number in the scale; I (Do), IV (Fa) and V (Sol), written in Roman numerals. Chords can be inverted or played in altered positions other than the root position and any note can be doubled in the chord, creating an octave.

Do	(1)	the Tonic	I
Fa	(4)	the Subdominant	IV
Sol	(5)	the Dominant	V

Another important chord is called the **seventh chord**, which forms the basis of moving from one key to another in transition. The most common seventh chord is the dominant 7th, which adds a minor third to a major triad. For example, a dominant seventh chord is created by adding a B♭ to the C major triad below.

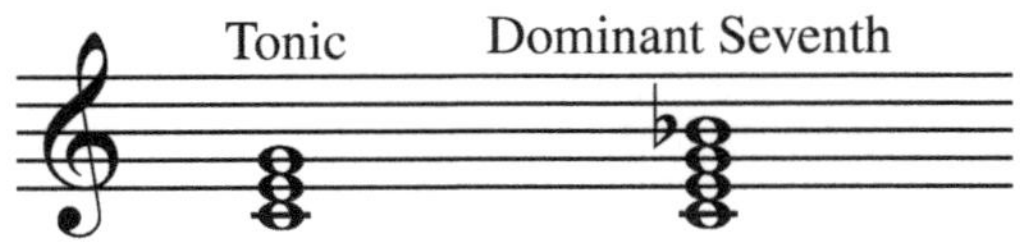

If the three notes in a triad are not played together as a chord, but played separately, the notes become an **arpeggio** (Do-Mi-Sol).

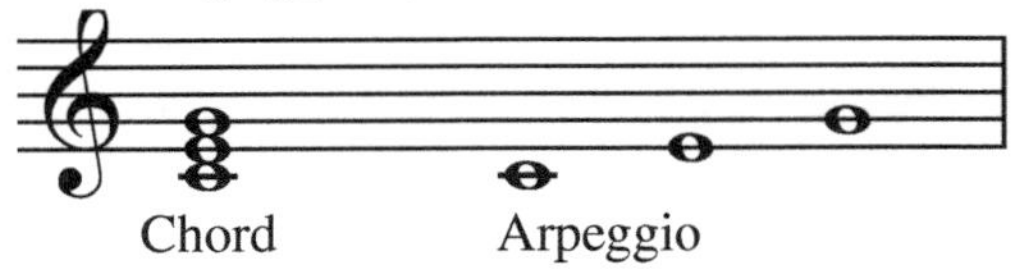

INSTANT HARMONY

Harmony can be added to a melody satisfactorily and quickly by adding an ostinato or descant to a familiar tune or by singing a round in two or more groups.

An **ostinato** is a short, repeated pattern that can be rhythmic or melodic. In the same key signature as the song itself, an ostinato might be a phrase taken directly from the song or an augmented pattern used in a creative way. Write your own simple ostinato for a song you already know well. Sing this ostinato with "Are You Sleeping" below.

Round/Canon - Harmony is heard when songs called rounds or canons are performed. One group of singers starts the song before another group comes in at an appointed time, also starting at the beginning. Try singing this familiar round as a class, divided into two to four groups as indicated for instant harmony. Find other rounds to perform.

The addition of a descant or countermelody to a melodic line is another way to create a harmony part. Usually sung above the original melody, the descant should be learned separately first, then added to the song as both are sung together. Create your own descant for a familiar song.

ACCOMPANIMENTS

Name ____

In a previous lesson, we learned about instruments that can play a melody (barred instruments, tone bells, recorders and keyboards.) To provide the musical background or **accompaniment** for a solo line, an instrument is required that can play several notes at once, or chords. In addition to a piano keyboard, the autoharp and guitar are popular chordal instruments used for playing accompaniments for singing.

To locate chord suggestions for a song accompaniment, look above the staff for single letters over the first beat of the measure. If no letter is shown above a measure, then the chord does not change from the previous measure.

AUTOHARP

One of the most popular accompaniment instruments is the autoharp, a member of zither family, originating in Bavaria. Chords are played by strumming the strings with the dominant hand while pushing labeled chord buttons with the other. A system of felt pads under the chord bars assures the accuracy of chords played by dampening all the strings except the desired pitches.

The autoharp can be played in the lap, on a table or held upright using just fingers or a plastic pick for steady strumming. A good way for young children to learn to play the autoharp is to work in partners with one person doing the strumming as the other pushes the appropriate chord buttons.

Shown in the example below is the chord arrangement for a fifteen bar autoharp with two rows of buttons to press. Notice how the I, IV and V chords in the most used keys are in close proximity to each other for easy access; (F, B♭ and C7 or C, F and G7).

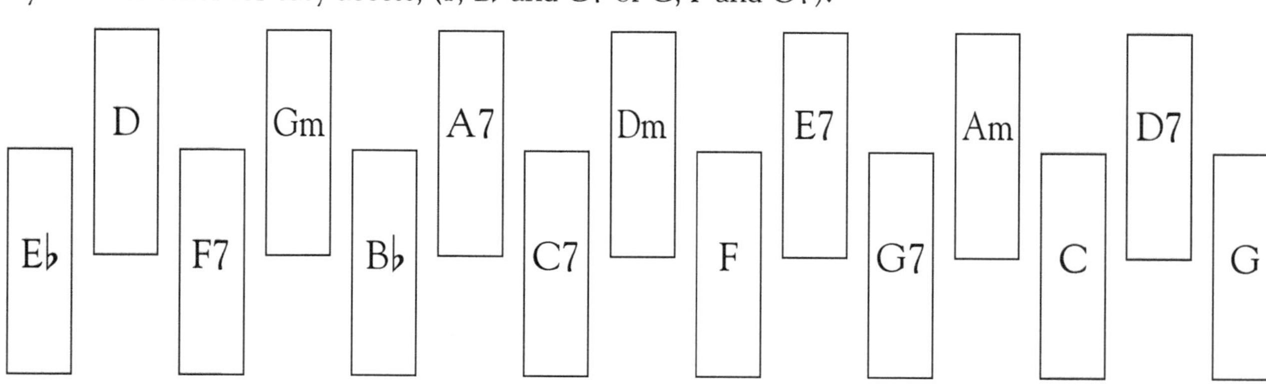

Play the suggested chord accompaniment for the following two-chord song, "The Yellow Rose of Texas," playing and strumming an autoharp as you sing.

GUITAR

Another popular accompaniment instrument is the **guitar**. For use with beginners in a classroom setting, classical guitars (acoustic) with nylon strings work well.

Unlike an autoharp with at least thirty-six strings to keep in tune, a guitar only has six strings to tune (E A D G B E). By turning the tuning pegs at the end of the neck, you can raise or lower the pitches. As shown below, the strings are numbered from the highest (#1) to the lowest (#6).

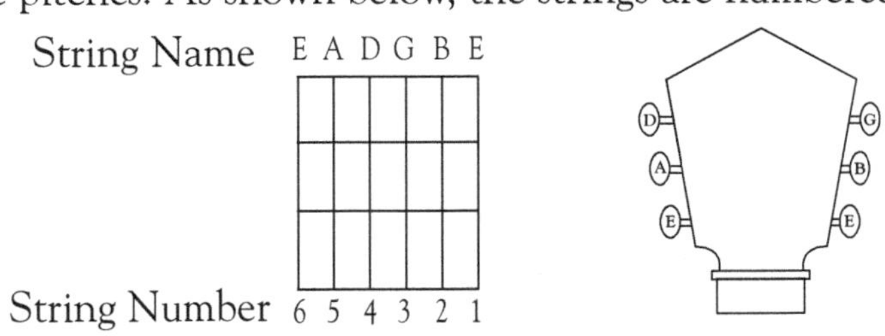

The techniques of *strumming* and *plucking* the strings are performed with the right hand as chords are formed with the left. The term *fretting* refers to pressing down on a string until it touches the board behind it. To play a chord on a guitar, simply press down on the individual strings indicated with the fingers of your left hand (see numbering for what fingers to use).

With your right hand, strum the strings that you have pressed and the ones with an 0 above them. If a string has an X above it, it is not used in that chord and should not be strummed.

Practice tuning a guitar using an accurately tuned piano or a pitch pipe as your guide. Start with a two-chord song to practice strumming, using G and D7 chords.

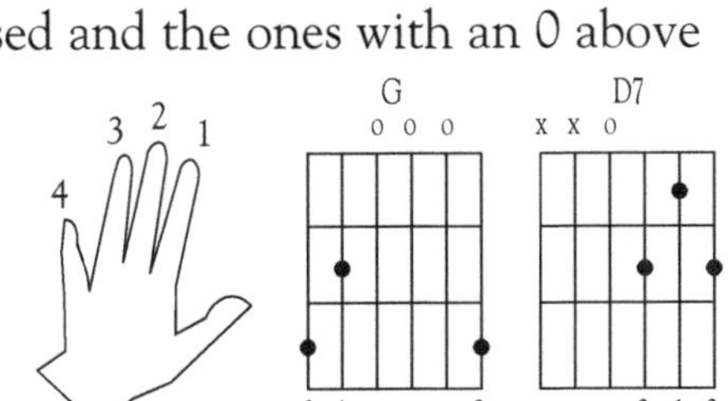

UKELELE

An accompaniment instrument that is easier to play than a guitar is the **ukelele**, a small Hawaiian instrument with only four strings, tuned to G (4) C (3) E (2) and A (1) or A (4) D (3) F# (2) and B (1).

24

MODULATION • TRANSPOSITION

Name ______________________________

The terms *modulation* and *transposition* both refer to the changing of musical keys, but with different purposes, as you will see.

MODULATION

From about the year 1700 on, some form of **modulation** or the changing of keys within a piece, occurred in most lengthy musical compositions. Many such pieces start and end in the same key, using passages in other keys for contrast and interest. Other pieces often modulate upwards from the original key as they progress toward completion.

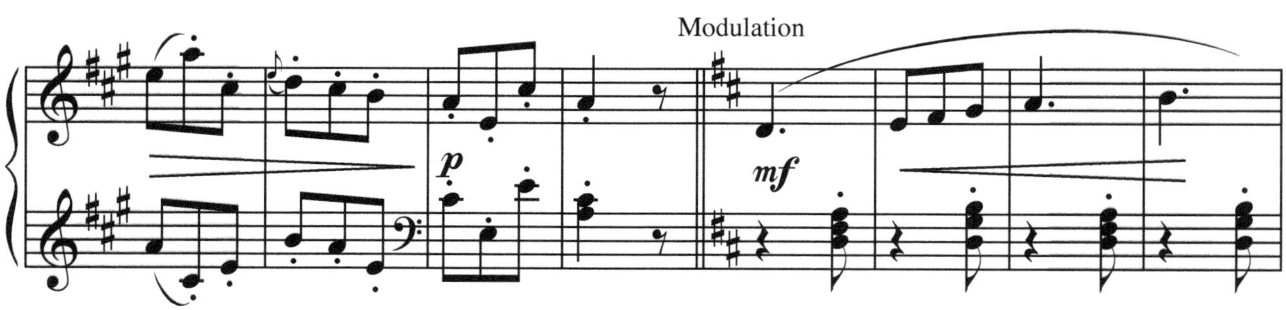

Key of ________ Key of ________

TRANSPOSITION

Transposition or transposing is the process of re-writing a whole piece in another key, making it conveniently higher or lower for a performer. In deciding whether or not to transpose a piece, the arranger would check the highest and lowest notes to determine how far these extremes could be moved and still be helpful.

Any piece in any key can be transposed if it is the same type of music such as a composition in a major key to another major key. It is necessary to keep the intervals accurate in changing keys, especially where accidentals are involved.

Look at the examples below to determine if they would be more comfortable to sing in a higher or lower key. To decide, first find and name the lowest note in the passage, then find and name the highest note. Notice where the remainder of the notes are. Are they in the middle, lower or upper range for the singer?

Could this song be raised easily, lowered or should it stay in the same key? __________

Give the reason for your decision.____

Could this song be raised easily, lowered or should it stay in the same key? __________

Give the reason for your decision. ____

START-TO-FINISH TRANSPOSING

1. Find the original key signature first.
2. Determine and write out the scale (major, minor or modal) on the staff.
3. Give each tone in the original key a number or solfège syllable identification.
4. Write out the scale in the new key with numbers or solfège syllable.
5. Determine the difference in the intervals to be moved, by half steps.
6. Assign the chords in the new key accurately from the original key.

Shown below is a passage of the patriotic song, "America," written in G Major. Your task is to re-write the same passage in C Major, a 4th higher, using the steps above to guide you. Check your work on a keyboard or other melody instrument for accuracy

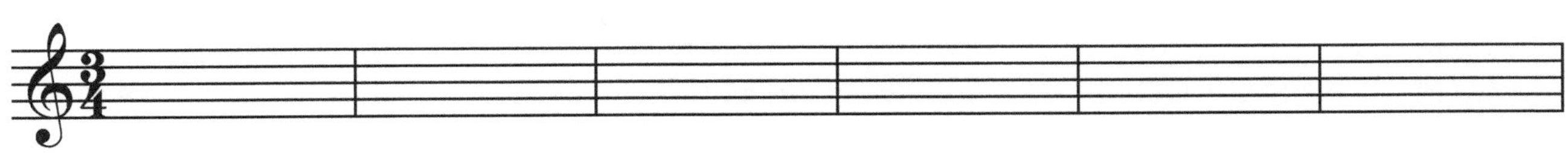

BONUS QUESTIONS

1. What is the difference between modulating and transposing? ____________________

____

____

2. Why is a clarinet called a "B-flat" clarinet? ____________________

____

____

MENTALITY • 23

25

GAMES

Name ______________________________

Playing team games using a melodic theme gives groups within the class and individual students the opportunity to show what you are learning about pitch and melody. Games played using **melody** as the theme, could involve reading solfège, identifying melodic patterns and finishing songs.

After you play each game suggested, move on to the **Bonus Level**, then create games of your own for teams to play within your class as you challenge each other.

GAME ONE: DRAWING DIAGRAMS

Materials: Melody bells, barred instruments or keyboard

Divide the class into two teams. Select two judges from each team who will determine if the answer drawn is correct. Next, the teacher or a volunteer from one team plays a three note melodic pattern. A member of the other team volunteers to draw a diagram on paper or chalkboard showing the contour of the pattern just played. If correct, that team gets a point, but if incorrect, the same pattern is played for the opposite team to try.

Ex. Play G A B Diagram:

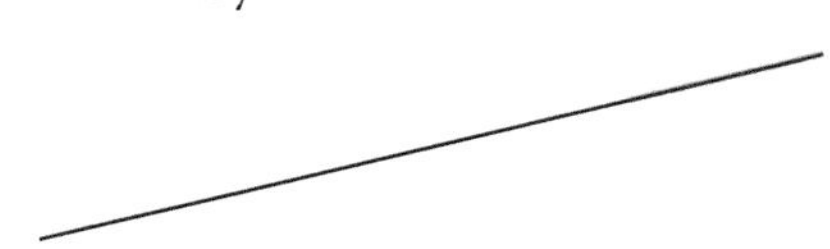

Play C E G Diagram:

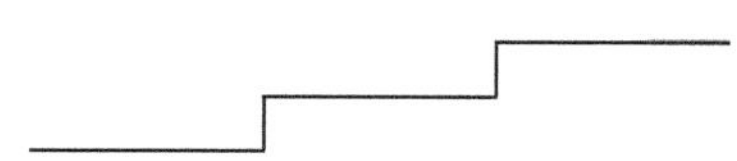

Bonus Level: Start with contour diagrams drawn by members of one team for the other to play matching pitches.

GAME TWO: LOCATING THE LAST NOTE

Materials: Melody bells, barred instruments or keyboard

The teacher or student volunteer plays the final phrase of a song, familiar or not, omitting the last note. Some samples are given for you. Call on volunteers from alternating teams to sing or play what they think the last note would be. After the students give their answer, the leader will play the phrase again, this time playing the correct pitch to end the song. Points are given for correct answers.

Bonus Level: Give bonus points if the volunteer can also sing the last note of the phrase as the correct solfège syllable.

1. 

2. 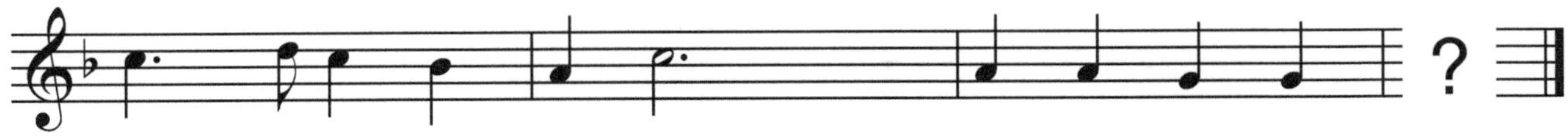

GAME THREE: VERY VOCAL

Materials: Melody bells, barred instruments or keyboard

Divide the class into two teams, lined up on each side of the room. The teacher or student leader plays a melodic pattern of three or four varied pitches within vocal range on a keyboard. The next person in line has only one chance to echo-sing the pattern on a neutral syllable. If the singer is not correct, the same melodic pattern is played for the next player on the other team to echo.

Bonus Level: Variation 1 – Use longer melodic patterns of five to eight notes to be echoed for more difficulty and memory. Variation 2 – Have the player identify the first note played by letter name or solfège syllable to see if the contestant can identify the remainder of the pattern.

GAME FOUR: PATCHWORK PARAGRAPHS

Divide the class into four equal groups, going to four locations in the classroom to work. Each group will need a chairman to keep the action going, a scribe to write down ideas and a reporter who will read the finished work to the class. Each small group must determine the words below from the names of the notes. Then they write a short paragraph incorporating those words. Every member of each group must contribute a line of the paragraph and all projects will be shared with the class when finished.

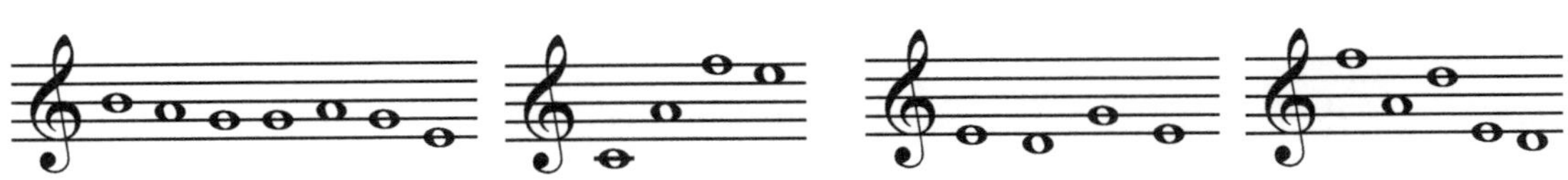

Bonus Level: Variation 1 – Each group makes up four words that can be spelled on the staff, giving them to another group for their writing. **Variation 2** – Instead of a paragraph, this round could include riddles or jokes, using the required words. **Variation 3** – Use words spelled on the bass clef instead of the treble clef.

Added Bonus: Set a timer for an appropriate number of minutes on any game to determine the limit of time for the activity to be concluded.

SONG SAMPLER

Name ______________________________

This lesson will take a look at the short melodic compositions called songs, which are usually accompanied. The words and music are equally important in song material, but the melodies make them memorable and unique.

Throughout the ages, the amount of song literature has grown, contributing to our culture. The following web introduces several familiar song styles considered to be culturally significant.

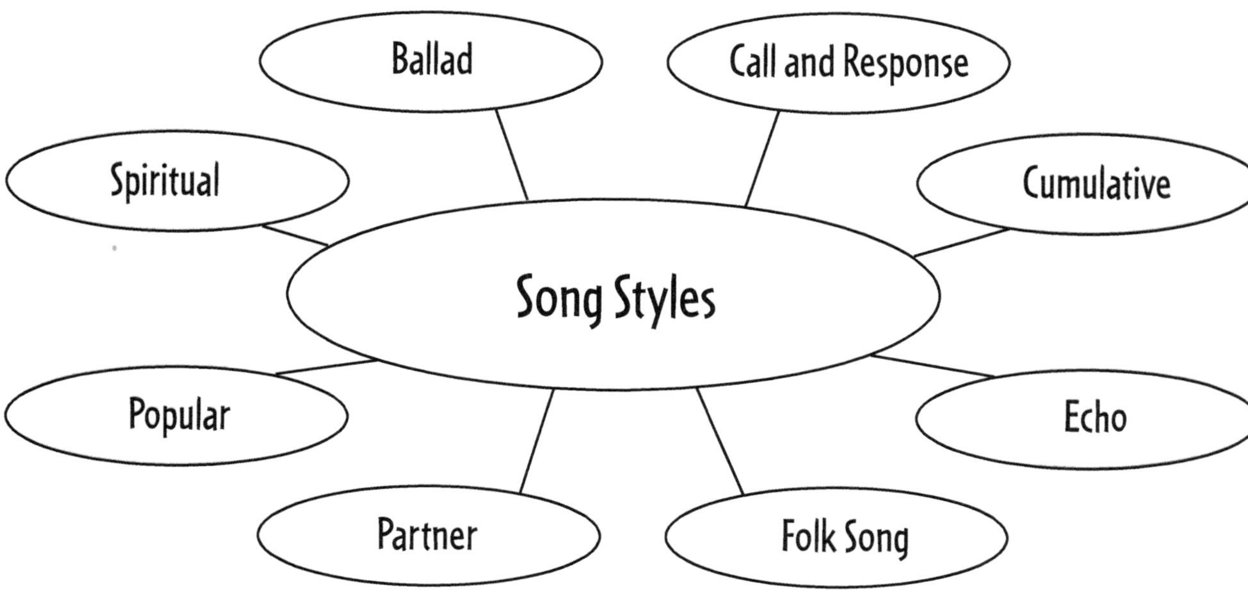

DEFINITIONS

1. **Ballad** – develops a story from verse to verse, using the same melody each time.
2. **Call and Response** – uses a soloist to sing a line with a group responding.
3. **Cumulative Song** – adds more tag words to each of several new verses.
4. **Echo Song** – one line is sung with the last note held, while another group sings the same line.
5. **Folk Song** – song material that is handed down from generation to generation by singing, usually without an identified composer.
6. **Partner Song** – two songs sung together with identical harmony structure and meter (or one song with verse and chorus sung together).
7. **Spiritual** – religious songs from the African heritage culture.
8. **Popular** – songs heard on the radio, television or modern performances, reflecting life situations and styles.

MATCHING

Using the following familiar songs, put a number from the definitions on page 52 in the appropriate blanks to categorize the song within a style:

_____ She'll Be Coming Around the Mountain

_____ My Aunt Came Back

_____ Old Joe Clark or Old Dan Tucker

_____ I'm Gonna Sing When the Spirit Says Sing

_____ Rock-a My Soul

_____ The Old Lady Who Swallowed a Fly

_____ Give My Regards to Broadway

_____ Who Built the Ark?

_____ John Henry or Casey Jones

Using a music book, make your own list of these categories, filling in the names of your favorite songs in each grouping.

PARTNER SONGS

Of the three basic music textures reviewed below, the third one refers to the concept of performing partner songs;

Monophonic Music (one sound) is the oldest type of music, consisting of a single melodic line without added parts or accompaniment.

Homophonic Music (joint sounds) consists of a single melodic line that is accompanied by chords.

Polyphonic Music (contrapuntal sounds) features two or more melodic lines having equal importance and significance performed simultaneously.

In order for the singing of partner songs to work successfully, both songs must be in the same key, with the same time signature, and the same length with the same chord structure. Practice performing partner songs in two groups, using these familiar tunes;

"Are You Sleeping? with "Hot Cross Buns"

"PawPaw Patch" with "Skip To My Lou"

"Liza Jane" with "Sandy Land"

"All Night, All Day" with "Swing Low, Sweet Chariot"

"Good Night Ladies" with "When the Saints Go Marching In"

BONUS QUESTIONS

1. Name five music elements that can be learned through the singing of songs. ______________

____

2. In your own words, define the word 'counterpoint'. ______________________________

____

MENTALITY • 25

27

MELODIC MASTERPIECE

Name ______________________________

Composers of great renown create melodies that live on through the ages, to be enjoyed by music lovers the world over. Many classical composers wrote melodies that are still popular in the present day. In one suite of pieces called "Peer Gynt," Edvard Grieg gave the world a great lasting gift.

BIOGRAPHICAL INFORMATION

Edvard Grieg (1843 – 1906) was born in Norway and got his first music training at age six from his mother, an accomplished musician. At nine years of age, he composed his first piece and was sent to study in Germany at age fifteen. In later years, he not only wrote music for the piano, but also expanded his work to include full orchestral scores.

One of Grieg's most successful orchestral works is the Peer Gynt Suite which includes "Morning," "Anitra's Dance" and "In the Hall of the Mountain King" as separate pieces. Premiered in 1876, the latter piece printed below began as music for the theatre, depicting trolls and gnomes in the story.

Play through the melodic line provided to see if you recognize this ageless music, and then number all the measures in order to answer the questions on the next page about the printed score.

IN THE HALL OF THE MOUNTAIN KING

FEEDBACK INFORMATION

1. In what key is this piece written? _____ How do you know? ____________________

   ____
2. What three kinds of notes are used in the entire piece? ____________________

   ____
3. Which measures are exactly like the beginning measures 1 – 7? ______________
4. What is the difference between line one and line two of the piece? ____________

   ____
5. Which measures are just like measures 9 – 12? ____________________
6. Which measures make up the coda? ____________________

BELOVED MELODIES

Below are beginning excerpts from pieces that are considered beloved by the world's music lovers. Play these melodies for your recognition. Do some research to determine the composer of each from the list provided below the examples.

Ex. 1 – "Traumerai" from *Scenes from Childhood*, Op. 15

Composed by ____

Ex. 2 - "Clair De Lune" from *Suite Bergamasque*

Composed by ____

Ex. 3 – "Ode to Joy" from *Symphony No. 9*

Composed by ____

Ex. 4 – "The Swan" from *Carnival of the Animals*

Composed by ____

(Claude Debussy, Ludwig van Beethoven, Camille Saint Saëns, Robert Schumann)

MENTALITY • 26

28

MELODIC MASTERPIECE

Name ______________________________

This lesson will introduce another master composer with a prolific career and an extraordinary gift for writing melodies. His music is still popular today and heard often in connection with ballet performances worldwide.

BIOGRAPHICAL INFORMATION

Peter (Pyotr) Ilyitch Tchaikovsky (1830 – 1893) was born in a small Russian town. Even though he played piano very early, his first serious interest in music came when his cousin taught him to modulate from one key to another, using only three chords.

In 1866, he was appointed a professor of music at the Moscow Conservatory. Included in his major works are *Sleeping Beauty* (1879), *Nutcracker Suite* (1892) and *Swan Lake* (1876). The theme from *Swan Lake* is printed below.

Play through the melodic line below to help you recognize this piece, then number all the measures in order to answer the questions on the next page about the printed music.

Locate and play orchestral recordings of all the selections in this and the previous lesson.

You can find them in the listening lessons from your textbook recordings or in collections by classical composers.

SWAN LAKE (ballet)
Theme

Pyotr Il'yich Tchaikovsky

FEEDBACK INFORMATION

1. In what key is this piece written? _____ How do you know? ____________________
2. Which measures repeat measures 1 – 4 closely? _____________ and _____________
3. Which measures feature an ascending conjunct melody? ________and ________
4. Which measures are exactly like measure 2? ________, _______ and _____________
5. Which accidentals are used in the piece? _________________________(Circle them)
6. On which solfège syllable does the piece start? _____ and end? _____

FAMILIAR MELODIES

Below are beginning excerpts from pieces that are considered familiar by the world's music lovers. Play these melodies for your recognition. Fill in the blanks with the title and composer from the list below.

1. – Title/Composer: ____

2. – Title/Composer: ____

3. – Title/Composer: ____

4. – Title/Composer: ____

Select from these choices to fill in the blanks for each piece:

"Lullaby" (Wiegenlied) by Johannes Brahms

"Pomp and Circumstance March No. 1" by Edward Elgar

Surprise Symphony (Second Movement Theme) by Franz Joseph Haydn

"Can Can" from *Orpheus in the Underworld* by Jacques Offenbach

MENTALITY • 27

29

COMPOSITION

Name ______________________________

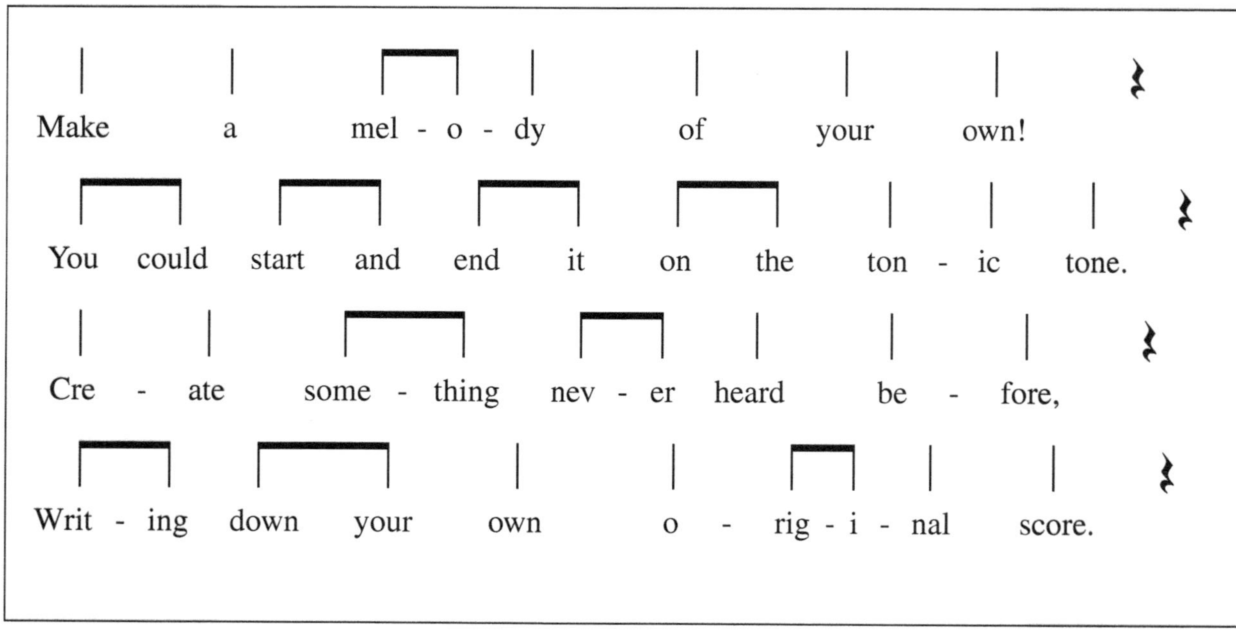

BE AN EDITOR

After learning many important things about the composition of melodies in these lessons, you should try your skill at creating a melody. Start by listening to and singing through the following examples on a neutral syllable (loo). Note the endings are omitted. Use the blank measures to write in your own suggestion on how the songs could be completed. Have the class sing your completed phrases with your leadership.

(two final measures)

(four final measures)

BE AN ARRANGER

When writing an original song, known concepts about melody, rhythm, key signatures, time signatures and harmony come into play. It is a simple process to make up songs in your mind, but notating your melody for others to sing or play is another story. An interesting melody features some contrast (using skips/steps and varying the direction) and repetition (notes or rhythm), finally coming to a close that sounds like an ending.

Use this simple phrase in example one and change it by changing the note values or rhythm to make a different sounding phrase in example two. Share your creation with the class.

1. 

2. 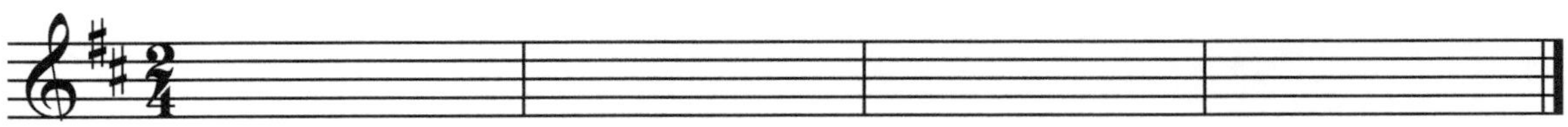

BE A COMPOSER

When writing a pentatonic melody, you eliminate much difficulty by using only five tones that all sound pleasant together. With either F (tonic or Do) G A C and D or C (tonic or Do) D E G and A as the only notes you will use, write an original four-measure melody below.

Next, use the poem found at the beginning of this lesson on page 58, and create a melody for it, individually or as a group. Decide upon a key signature and using $\frac{4}{4}$ meter, try your skills at setting a poem to music.

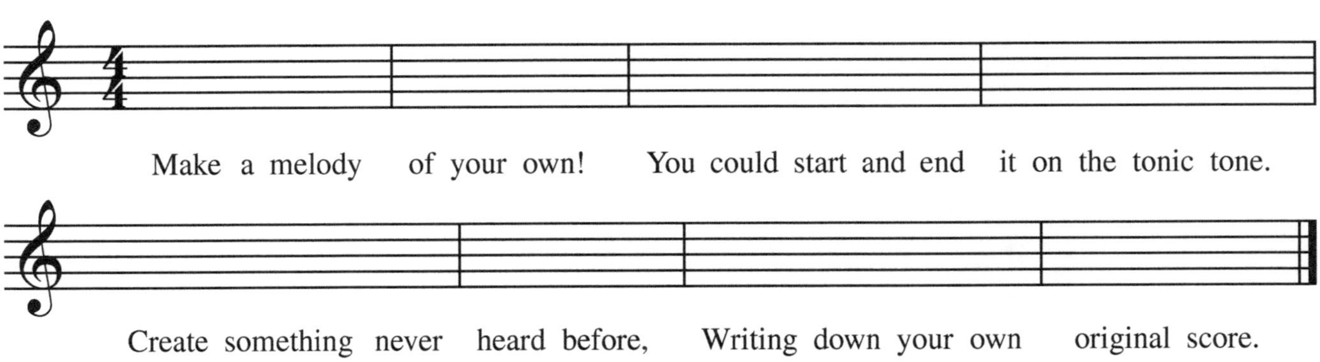

MELODIC MASTERY 30

PUTTING IT ALL TOGETHER!

Name ______________________________

Choose the best answer for each of the following questions:

_____1. Pitches that ascend move
- a. downward c. steadily
- b. upward d. around

_____2. A pentatonic scale has
- a. 8 tones c. 5 tones
- b. 4 tones d 12 tones

_____3. A span of eight notes is
- a. a phrase c. a motive
- b. an octave d. an ostinato

_____4. This sign (♭) is
- a. a flat c. an interval
- b. a sharp d. a natural

_____5. A sequential tone series is a
- a. scale c. section
- b. phrase d. motive

_____6. An accidental is used to
- a. punctuate c. repeat
- b. change pitch d. accent

_____7. A melody that moves stepwise is
- a. conjunct c. disjunct
- b. repeated d. sharp

_____8. Vibrations determine
- a. phrasing c. pitch
- b. accents d. volume

_____9. Descending pitches move
- a. across c. upward
- b. downward d. higher

____10. A melodic climax is
- a. a highpoint c. triple
- b. sharp d. a beat

____11. An example of triple meter is
- a. 2/4 c. 4/4
- b. 6/8 d. 3/4

____12. A 'ta-titi-ta-titi' pattern is
- a. ♩ ♩ ♫ ♩ c. ♫ ♩ ♫ ♩
- b. ♫ ♩ ♩ ♩ d. ♩ ♫ ♩ ♫

____13. Notes with two flags are
- a. eighth notes c. half notes
- b. sixteenth notes d. quarter notes

____14. The top number of a time signature refers to
- a. beats c. barlines
- b. flats d. repeats

____15. Common time is
- a. 2/4 c. 6/8
- b. 3/4 d. 4/4

____16. The 'cut time' symbol is
- a. ♭ c. 𝄵
- b. 𝄴 d. ♯

____17. The 'natural' symbol is
- a. ♭ c. 𝄵
- b. 𝄴 d. ♮

____18. A pentatonic scale is
- a. DRMFS c. DRMSD
- b. DRMSL d. DRFLD

____19. The relative minor of the F Major scale is
- a. d minor c. a minor
- b. g minor d. c minor

____20. An example of a duple meter is
- a. 2/4 c. 6/8
- b. 3/4 d. 4/4

____21. Cancel a sharp or flat with
- a. ♯ c. 𝄐
- b. 𝄵 d. ♮

____22. A musical sentence is a
- a. phrase c. accent
- b. line d. scale

____23. A tetrachord is made up of
a. 4 tones c. 6 tones
b. 5 tones d. 8 tones

____24. A key signature with two sharps is
a. G Major c. D Major
b. A Major d. C Major

____25. The distance between two pitches is
a. an accidental c. a scale
b. an interval d. a signature

____26. An example of an Orff instrument is
a. flute c. piano
b. xylophone d. guitar

____27. A fifth interval is
a. C to F c. C to G
b. C to A d. C to D

____28. Two black piano keys come between
a. C and E c. F and B
b. D and F d. A and C

____29. The left hand plays the top of a
a. piano c. xylophone
b. recorder d. metallophone

____30. The first solfège pitches to learn are
a. SM c. DR
b. LS d. MF

____31. The largest recorder is called the
a. soprano c. tenor
b. alto d. bass

____32. The enharmonic note for G♯ is
a. A♭ c. B♭
b. D♭ d. E♭

____33. Which word could be spelled on a staff?
a. purse c. wallet
b. baggage d folio

____34. Which of the following is not a chordal instrument used to provide accompaniment?
a. recorder c. piano
b. guitar d. autoharp

____35. The pitch of a tuning fork is
a. A440 c. A880
b. A660 d. A330

____36. 'G Clef' is another name for the
a. keyboard c. bass
b. treble d. scale

____37. The key with no sharps or flats is
a. E Major c. A Major
b. C Major d. D Major

____38. Lines of the staff are numbered from
a. the top c. the side
b. the bottom d. the middle

____39. The fourth line of the treble clef is
a. F c. B
b. G d. D

____40. The key of A Major has
a. 2 sharps c. 3 sharps
b. 4 sharps d. 5 sharps

____41. The key of A flat Major has
a. 2 flats c. 3 flats
b. 4 flats d. 5 flats

____42. Ledger lines are
a. curvy c. pointed
b. not on the staff d. not needed

____43. An autoharp is played by
a. blowing c. strumming
b. hitting d. bowing

____44. Chordal notation is found
a. under the staff c. above the staff
b. in a box d. on the staff

____45. 'F Clef' is another name for the
a. keyboard c. bass
b. treble d. scale

____46. The fourth line of the 'F Clef' is
a. F c. D
b. G d. E

____47. To play G on a recorder, you use
a. right hand only c. left hand only
b. both hands d. no hands

____48. A repeat sign looks like this.
a. ♯ c. 𝄐
b. 𝄢 d. 

____49. The process of changing keys is called
a. shifting c. writing
b. modulation d. training

____50. The term for a combination of sounds is
a. harmony c. pentatonic
b. solfège d. melody

ANSWERS

SECTION 1: MELODIC MOTIF

Page 3:
(Bonus Questions)
1. Composer: Ludwig van Beethoven
   Title of Piece: "Symphony No. 5 in C minor"
2. (Ex.) Melody is the soul of music because of its qualities of recognition and remembrance.

Page 5:
(Matching)
1. h 2. g 3. f 4. c 5. j
6. i 7. d 8. b 9. a 10. e

(Scrambled Terms)
1. INTERVAL 2. CONTOUR 3. PHRASE
4. MOTIVE 5. NOTATION

(In these blanks)
a. 3 b. 2 c. 1 d. 2 e. 3

(Fill in the Blanks)
1. pentatonic 2. interval 3. pitch
4. Range 5. accidentals

(Bonus Questions)
1. conjunct = stepwise, disjunct = skipwise
2. 4th and 7th

SECTION 2: MELODIC METHODS

Page 7
(Same/Different)
Ex. 2, Ex. 3, Ex. 1

(Bonus Questions)
1. An oscilloscope is a instrument which shows variations in electrical currents on a screen and is used to tune musical instruments to a true pitch.
2. Perfect (absolute) pitch refers to the ability to name or sing a particular pitch without any outside reference in preparation.

Page 9
1. Both
(Bonus Questions)
1. Climax (peak of interest) = land of the (free)

Page 11
(Dotted Notes)
𝅗𝅥. = 3 beats ♪. = 1½ beats ♩. = 1½ beats ♩. = 1½ beats

(Tied Notes)
𝅝‿♩ = 5 beats 𝅝‿𝅝 = 8 beats

(Bonus Questions)
1.

2. (Circled above)

Page 12
(Practice Makes Perfect)
3/2: 3 = three beats in each measure
2 = a half note gets one beat

3/4: 3 = three beats in each measure
4 = a quarter note gets one beat

6/8: 6 = six beats in each measure
8 = an eighth note gets one beat

Page 13
(Match Them Up)

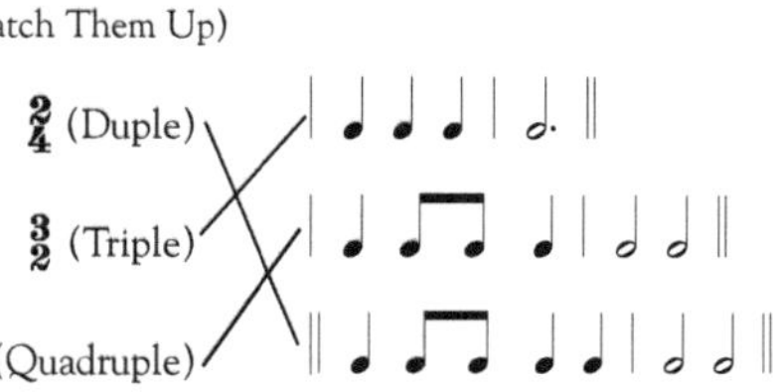

(Fill in the Time)
4/4, 3/8, 2/4

Page 14
(Major Scales)

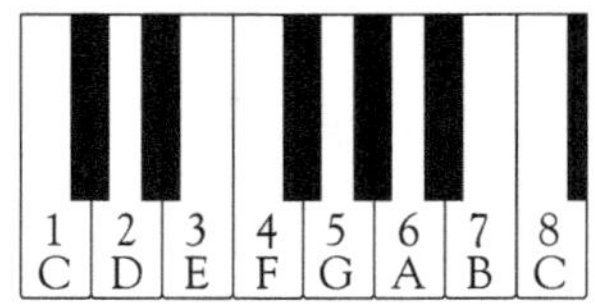

Page 15

C D E G A	F G A C D	G A B D E
C Pentatonic	F Pentatonic	G Pentatonic

(Bonus Question)
A tetrachord is a scale consisting of four sequential tones, devised by the Greeks. A lower tetrachord plus an upper tetrachord make up a major (eight tone) scale.

Page 16
(Sharps)
Ex. A♯, F♯, D♯

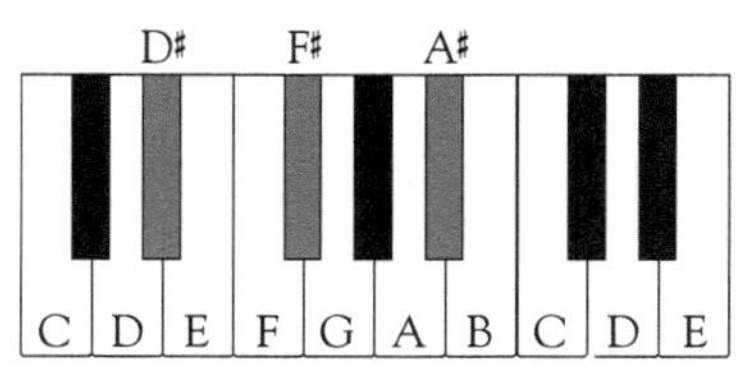

Page 17
(Flats)
Ex. A♭, E♭, D♭

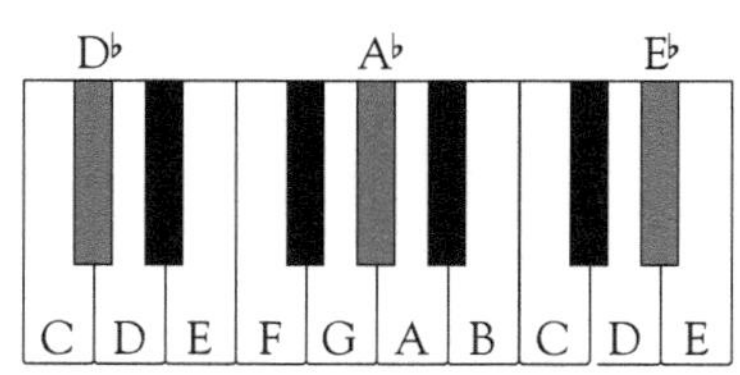

(What is Wrong Here?)
Song 1 – Sweet land "of" liberty – B note should be lowered one half step
Song 2 – Po- "ny" – F note should be raised one half step
Song 3 - "All the" – B notes should be lowered one half step
Enharmonic – F♯, G♭

(Bonus Questions)
1. Yes, F
2. Yes, B

Page 19
(Interesting Intervals)

5th	3rd	7th	4th	Octave	2nd	6th
H	M	H	H	H	M	M

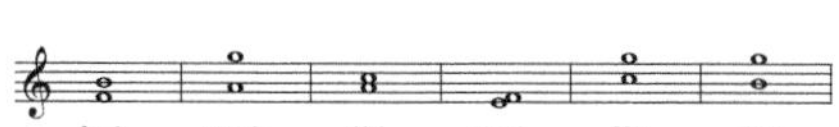

(Bonus Questions)
1. 5th 2. 4th 3. 6th 4. 3rd

MELODIC MASTERY TEST

Page 20
1. accidental: signs that raise or lower a pitch.

   interval: distance between two notes.

   octave: interval of eight scale degreees

   phrase: a musical sentence or thought
2. Ex. 1 - disjunct, Ex. 2 - conjunct
3.

4. ta ti-ti ta ti-ti
5. 3 = three beats in each measure
   4 = a quarter note gets one beat

Page 21
6. C = 4/4
7. ¢ = 2/2
8. duple, triple, quadruple
9. A B C D E F G
10. C D E F G A B C
11. relative, harmonic, melodic
12. 4th and 7th
13.

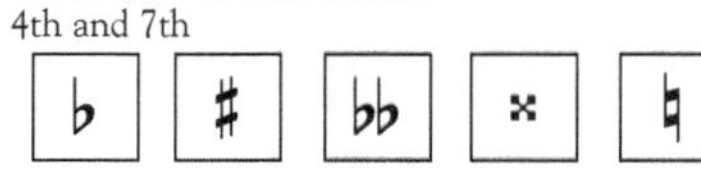

flat sharp dbl flat dbl sharp natural

14. A motive is a short distinctive melodic pattern.
15. 5th, 2nd, Octave, 7th

SECTION 3 - MELODIC MATERIALS

Page 23

(Bonus Questions)
1. 'fi' between fa and sol, 'si' between sol and la, 'ta' between la and ti
2. Do, Mi, Sol, high Do

Page 25
(Bonus Questions)
1. Pentatonic

Page 26
(Sharps)
G, D, A, E, B, F♯, C♯

Page 27
(Flats)
F, B♭, E♭, A♭, D♭, G♭, C♭

(Bonus Questions)
1. No, it is used in the music to cancel out sharps and flats.
2. B♯ = C, C♭ = B, E♯ = F

Page 28

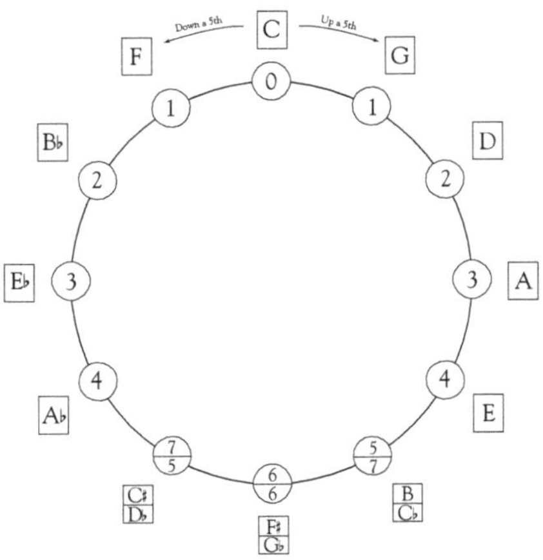

Page 29
(Major Vs. Relative Minor)
1. a minor 2. d minor 3. b minor 4. f♯ minor

(Who Has the Keys?)
a. A/f♯ b. B♭/g c. A♭/f d. D/b

(Bonus Questions)
1. 3 flats (B♭, E♭ and A♭)
2. 6 sharps (F♯, C♯, G♯, D♯, A♯ and E♯)

Page 31
(Spell Words)
a. D E A F b. B E A D
c. B A D G E d. B A G G A G E

Page 33
Ex. Line 1

Rhythm ti ti ta ta ta ta ta ta-ah ta ta ta-ah ta
Solfège M F S S D' T L D' S M S L
Note kind E E Q Q Q Q Q H Q Q H Q
Letter names E F G G C B A C G E G A

Ex. Line 2

Ex. (Line 2)
Rhythm ta-ah-ah ti ti ta ta ta ta ta ta-ah ta ta ta-ah ta ta-ah-ah
Solfège R M F S S D' T L D' L S R' L D'
Note kind DH E E Q Q Q Q Q H Q Q H Q DH
Letter names D E F G G C B A C A G D B C

(Bonus Question)
G Clef – because the symbol centers around the second line (G) of the treble clef
F Clef – because the symbol centers around the fourth line (F) of the bass clef

Page 35
(Sharps)

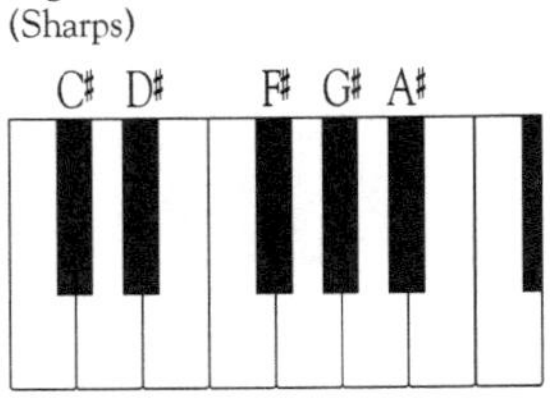

(Flats)

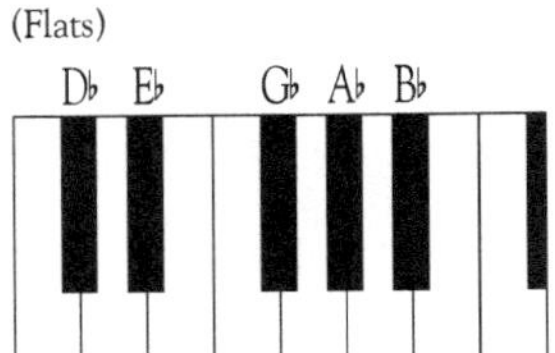

(True or False)
1. F 2. T 3. T 4. F 5. F
(Bonus Questions)
1. A harpsichord has hammers instead of felt covered mallets and cannot play louder when struck harder.
2. An electronic synthesizer is an instrument that can produce, modify and organize sounds by electronic means, controlling the frequency and intensity of those sounds.

Page 37
(Bonus Questions)
1. raise
2. A440 – used for tuning instruments and determining standard pitch.

Page 39

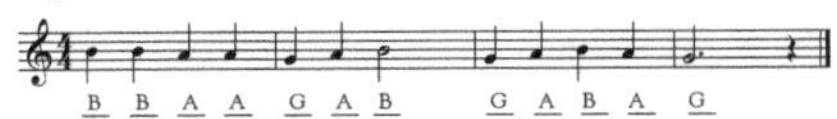

(Bonus Question)
1. for more accurate tuning of the note "F"

MELODIC MASTERY TEST

Page 40
(Matching)
1. f 2. e 3. a 4. c 5. d 6. g
7. b

2. a. A C E b. F E D
c. A D D E D d. F A C E D

3. a. F/d b. G/e
c. E♭/c d. E/c♯

Page 41
4. a. C♯, D♯, E♯
b. E♭, D♭, C♭
c. A♭, A♯
d. Soprano, alto, tenor and bass
e. little finger of the left hand

5. a. D R M F b. R F S D
c. F L F S d. L F R D

6.

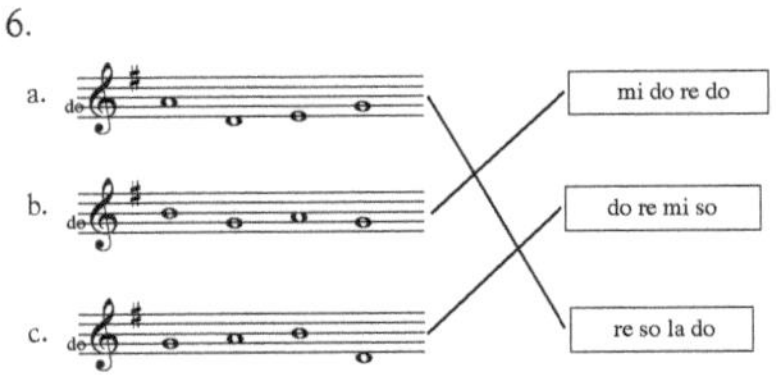

7. (treble) G A B C D E F, D C B A G F E
(bass) B C D E F G A, F E D C B A G

8.

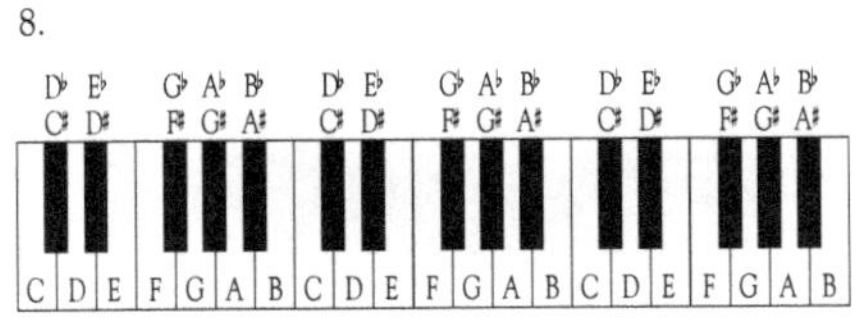

SECTION 4: MELODIC MENTALITY

Page 43
Ex. 1

Song Title: "Michael, Row the Boat Ashore"

Ex. 2

(Bonus Questions)
1. Playing by ear is the ability to play a familiar song on the first try without reading the printed music.
2. Solfege or solfa

Page 44
(Building triad chords)

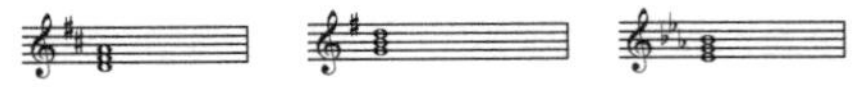

Page 48
(Modulation) Key of A Major Key of D Major
(Transposition)
Ex. 1 - This song could be raised and still be in a comfortable range for a singer.

Page 49
Ex. 2 – This song should stay in the same key because of the wide range.

(Start to Finish Transposing)

Ex. 2
(Bonus Questions)
1. Modulating means to change key signatures within a piece, while transposing is rewriting an entire piece in another key.
2. A clarinet is called a B flat clarinet because it is a transposing instrument with transposed notes to play.

Page 51
Ex. 1 – last note is G
Ex. 2 – last note is F
(Game Four Words)
B A G G A G E, C A F E, E D G E, F A D E D

Page 53
(Matching)
3, 4, 1, 7, 6, 3, 8, 2, 5

(Bonus Questions)
1. 5 Elements = (Ex.) beat, rhythm, phrasing, melodic direction and form
2. Counterpoint is a method where two melodies are played or sung simultaneously.

Page 55
(Feedback Information)
1. (b minor) – from key signature, first note of piece and letter clue above the first beat
2. eighth notes, quarter notes and half notes
3. measures 17-23
4. line two is a repeat of line one, done an octave higher
5. measures 13-16
6. measures 25-28

(Beloved Melodies)
Ex. 1 – Robert Schumann
Ex. 2 – Claude Debussy
Ex. 3 – Ludwig van Beethoven
Ex. 4 – Camille Saint Saëns

Page 57:
(Feedback Information)
1. (a minor) – from key signature, first note of piece and letter clue above the first beat
2. measures 5-8 and 18-21
3. measures 9 and 13
4. measures 6 and 19 and 23
5. B flat, B natural, F♯ and G♯
6. Sol, Do

(Familiar Melodies)
Ex. 1 – *Surprise Symphony* (Second Movement Theme) by Franz Joseph Haydn
Ex. 2 – "Lullaby" (Wiegenlied) by Johannes Brahms
Ex. 3 – "Can Can" from *Orpheus in the Underworld* by Jacques Offenbach
Ex. 4 – "Pomp and Circumstance March No.1" by Edward Elgar

Page 60 – 61:
(Putting It All Together)

1. b	2. c	3. b	4. a	5. a
6. b	7. a	8. c	9. b	10. a
11. d	12. d	13. b	14. a	15. d
16. c	17. d	18. b	19. a	20. a
21. d	22. a	23. a	24. c	25. b
26. b	27. c	28. a	29. b	30. a
31. d	32. a	33. b	34. a	35. a
36. b	37. b	38. b	39. d	40. c
41. b	42. b	43. c	44. c	45. c
46. a	47. c	48. d	49. b	50. a

ABOUT THE AUTHOR

Betsy Henderson is the Fine Arts Coordinator for Garland ISD, Garland, Texas, where she directs the award-winning Garland All-City Girls Choir. With degrees from Midwestern State University and the University of North Texas, she has served as elementary state chairmen for both the Texas Music Educators Association and the Texas Choral Directors Association. An author of the music textbook series, *Share the Music*, published by Macmillan/McGraw-Hill Company, Betsy has also written *The Composers Special Guide*, and *Thirty Days to Rhythm*, published by Hal Leonard.